Returning to America

The book that will change America

By Mark Dean

For all who love America the Beautiful and want to keep it, welcome the book worth more than any book, event, interest, or material good of recent time. This book is about saving the nation of your dreams and all you value within it – quality of life, family, children, livelihood, economy, and future. This book contains unprecedented answers for keeping everything most important!

It is not about distractions, discouragement, problems, or defeat! It is about empowerment to restore the nation of our dreams in precisely the ways which fill every wish. This is also about taking simple steps within our grasp to do it rather than let everything go to failure.

For every hope and dream in America, welcome the plan to restore the nation of our dreams so every dream is attainable. All great success happens with a game plan. Until now, America was filled with desire but not the simple steps to achieve it. This is that plan for benefiting every American most by restoring the greatest nation. All well-wishing in the world won't change it. Telling many others about the message in this book will. This is that plan like no other has offered, a real game plan for America the beautiful!

Some think it's ridiculous to believe we can change direction. The numbers prove otherwise! The numbers are OVERWHELMINGLY in favor of the MAJORITY. It's 300 million to only 536 failed politicians. We'd be ridiculous for not changing direction since our other option is to continue the current direction leading us to the worst poverty by competing with billions across the globe earning $2.00 per day! Sitting idle while this happens is like staying in the middle of the road while a semi-truck is coming down the road!

Tell many about this mission, this book, and the USAFreedom.us website so freedom's children don't take the hit from our indifference and failure to act!

P.S. – Follow this plan to awaken the giant and then the system in Washington will change.

© 2007 Mark Dean
ISBN: 978-1-4303-2094-4

Scripture references are taken from the King James Version of the Bible.

Printed in the United States of America.

The content of this book is the sole opinion of its author and may not necessarily reflect all of the opinions of its sponsors.

Contents

Dedication

This book is dedicated first to my father and late mother who made all things possible. Their love established for me confidence to pursue all I desire in knowledge and opportunity. Their example gave me understanding to enjoy citizenship with others in this life as well as in the next one to follow. Their roles gave me the means to move forward with certainty that I am loved and capable to do for others the good my parents have done for me. This book is also dedicated to each and every individual along the way who has contributed richly to my life with all from a simple smile to most empowering insight. For the love and good will, I am most grateful and wanting to repay through the pages of this book.

Preface

Welcome everything good opposite to bad politics. Welcome everything intelligent opposite to every great failure and expense. Welcome the brightest answers opposite to America's worst nightmare. *Returning to America* is America's great political solution. It is also America's great personal empowerment solution for richest personal rewards.

This book describes the means for America's majority of 300 million-strong to reclaim the power of the majority and dramatically improve the state and future of America. This is different from the other view that nothing can be done to save America from the worst to come. Much can be done. This book is proof of that! Make no mistake. Idle response and attitude of defeat are made to reap the worst nightmare. The other view shows for certain there are answers opposite to every problem. This view makes all things possible. The answers come from choosing a path where each step taken is progress forward in the direction we want to go. There is nothing new. All that remains is how to improve the nation of our dreams in the same way every goal is achieved.

The primary focus of this book is not to define America's problems in comprehensive detail. It does shed light on most serious ones and assumes others are already all too well known. More important, *Returning to America* is really about empowerment. It describes the steps required for winning in every way including ending global competition with billions of workers across the globe earning $2.00 per day. Currently, a minority of power grabbers is working to transfer the people's state to a corporate state and a foreign state. This makes it easy for the worst power grab of all. You will find in this book why current trends are giving the power to corporate power grabbers and more significantly to communist China, but not if America's majority awakens to very simple realities for winning back America from the few right at home. Find dramatic and powerful answers in this book for saving America from the worst to come.

While *Returning to America* identifies the largest trends threatening the future of all Americans and the entire free world, it also provides the solutions on the other side far more potent and appealing than every great failure and expense happening now on the opposite side. For a 300 million-majority, the insights in this book are the answer! Topics include –

The Great Majority Power Move – how 300 million-strong can reclaim power with a stronger voice than less than 600 souls in Washington

How to return to traditional values rather than live in poverty to the lead of corporate exploitation by the few and communist economics

How to expose corruption in Washington and hold public officials publicly accountable

How to replace big-money campaigns and big-money corruption with publicly funded debates

How to end the sale of the people's state to a corporate state, a foreign state, and a communist state with talk of treason

How to restore the greatest nation

How to prosper a nation opposite to every failure and expense

Returning to America will inspire your finest performance to win convincingly in the ways which make one and all whole in a nation where policy needs repair and the best of human spirit working together can do it! 300 million-strong have power over less than 600 souls in Washington!

Returning to America is the answer!

P.S. – With the broad content of this book, you may choose to read it either cover to cover or by favorite topic.

The Majority's Great-unanswered Questions

Who will lead? Will less than 600 in Washington lead or will 300 million lead? Will their be enough teamwork from the majority to lead or will less than 600 hundred in Washington lead and dominate up to 300 million slaves? Will the people's state lead or will the corporate state lead? Will sovereign interests lead or will foreign interests lead? Will America the beautiful lead or will communist China lead? Will greedy corporate executives lead or will China's communist party with military might lead? Will America regain strength by doing what is smart or will communist China simply take over because the majority isn't smart enough to repeat simple empowerment moves?

Bonus question: Will free-world countries see what is going on and team up to save economies around the world from communist economics which can ruin economies and human lifestyle everywhere?

One of two events WILL occur. Either communist China will emerge as the world power with the full influence of communism or there will be enough resolve in America to change direction and stop that from happening. America's great majority will either gain the resolve and power to protect America's borders and reshape the greatest nation or continue to be modeled after communist China. Either way, America's majority is responsible for the outcome by the sheer power they hold. 300 million have far more power than less than 600 in Washington. The answer comes from repeating simple, easy-to-do moves! By majority resolve, empowering insight, and like-minded decision, the majority can be the ultimate leaders and winners. They will be the ultimate decision makers. This is government of the people.

For those wanting change, it won't happen without a plan of action. For those who think it can't be done, our majority outnumbers politicians 500,000 to one. The numbers are dramatically in our favor. If we think failure, we will reap failure. If we think victory, we will reap victory. We reap what we think. Most important is how to think as one! Returning to America is the means to do it.

The Goal

The goal is to return America to a people's state rather than a corporate state, foreign state, communist state, or political state led by less than 600 politicians in Washington. The goal includes a comprehensive and unprecedented system of change. This change is most desired, most tangible, and right within our grasp of 300 million souls! 300 million Americans compared to 600 politicians is 500,000 to every one politician. Successful achievement of this goal will impact all of the future most favorably for people everywhere! This is the age-old story of good over evil. This is also the goal with greatest reward for all who pursue it. This is the same the few in Washington are completely ignoring. This is also the same America was built on and can repeat again simply by repeating success. This goal is not about seeking riches on the other side of the globe. This is about enjoying the ultimate opportunities right at home and within our borders by making America everything it can be opposite to obvious failure! Returning to America is also about surrounding our lives with wealth on the inside and success on the inside to reshape the nation of our dreams in ways of greatest significance. The great majority can win most desirable change by repeating as one some concepts within this book. The goal includes the sum total of its parts. Those parts are listed below -

Replace big-money politicians and big-money campaigns with publicly funded debates. This will bring back a representative form of government representing the people's state and not a corporate state, a political state, or a foreign state! It will also end the flow of big money!

Replace failing leaders with successful leaders who have new direction and refreshing intelligence to restore the greatest nation!

Protect America's borders and manage America's economy to serve America. This includes the model of Sweden where workers work one job and have five weeks paid vacation. This means changing the economic model following the lead of communist China, slave labor, and failure in every way. It also means following the model of Sweden where political leaders are smart enough to look after the needs of their own country and put the needs of their own country first. It also means restoring the greatest nation to model freedom and prosperity for the world again as it did before!

Expose corrupt leaders in Washington and end their corruption by improving the system of public accountability!

Activate the 300 million-majority to reclaim government of the people by repeating together simple, easy-to-do power moves which give the majority overwhelming power over less than 600 in Washington!

Revitalize America's economy by going opposite to every great failure and expense!

This book describes how to achieve the above and more to restore America the Beautiful once again as a model of freedom and prosperity!

Successful achievement of this goal is the ultimate way to success in every way! The opposite way loses in every way!

P.S. – End the myth that all will be fine by simply electing one more republican or democrat into office!

P.P.S. – Tell the people of Mexico to end slave labor in Mexico so they don't bring slavery to America and contaminate America with the same human failure they need to fix in Mexico!

P.P.P.S – The U.S. Constitution never gave 536 failed politicians power to sell government of the people. Government of the people is about 300 million having the personal character to live in the land of their choosing by telling the few how to run government. The laws of treason are the people's laws to protect the people from politicians gone bad! Will 300 million rule or will they live in poverty and slavery for lack of leadership to rule their lives, laws, government, and destiny?

The Great Majority Power Move

The Great Majority Power Move is the means for 300 million Americans to reclaim America the Beautiful for all of freedom's children. It is the message and means not one American had before! Now each of 300 million can. Not one had before a message and a comprehensive plan with power to change the nation. Not one had before a website, a book, and a game plan to do it. Not one had before a potent voice beyond big money advertising and 536 failed politicians to reclaim the nation of their dreams. For 300 million, no longer does it make sense to be without the message. Reclaim the nation of your dreams from America's worst nightmare! Welcome The Great Majority Power Move!

The Great Majority Power Move is a real grassroots campaign. No longer does it make sense to look to 536 failed politicians. The power is in "we the people!" 300 million repeating the same voice together can end the worst nightmare – the few selling the majority to corporate exploitation, communist economics, and the worst poverty to come. The details of this plan give 300 million-strong overwhelming power over 536 failed politicians. It happens by repeating the same great power move millions of times over to change direction. The results can be overwhelming simply by doing it together. This is the REAL way to change. The majority is the right group to change it. Politicians in Washington won't. They are already proven failures. This plan provides the means to do it with simple, easy-to-repeat ways for achieving the goal. The results are opposite to the poverty plan in place now leading America's work force to poverty with billions across the globe earning $2.00 per day. Under the current plan, ruthless exploitation, price gouging, deep poverty, and the worst nightmare will continue to change the face of America forever. The Great Majority Power Move is the answer. No other plan will reward you more and no other means more to your future!

End the current corrupt election system so the majority can elect a new brand of leaders and a new kind of president who serves the majority!

It happens with a great majority power move! Under the current election system, America's presidential choices are limited to the few stars of failure from two failed political parties. This is the few in Washington with millions of dollars to start. Once these softies get in, their loyalties go to big money interests that get them there. This is not representative form of government and government of the people as described in our U.S. Constitution! This failed system must end! For this reason, the presidential race I was considering, I have dropped for a more fundamental task – replacing the failed election system.

The following is included in the Great Majority Power Move.

End corruption in government within one year. This can happen as soon as the majority takes the simple steps below to regain power. Sooner is better than later so we don't elect another incompetent president to lead us deeper into communist economics. We can't take four more years of the same. Our new leadership must have intelligence and courage to end communist economics in America.

Replace big money campaigns and big money corruption with publicly funded debates. This will give the majority presidential choices based on content rather than big pocket books!.

Talk of treason for those in government who continue to sell off the people's sovereign state to a corporate state and a foreign state led by communist China. The Great Majority Power Move is the answer for exposing and eliminating the worst offenders.

Empower the majority with a promotion campaign operated by the majority for the majority so the majority of 300 million-strong have the means to reclaim America from the few selling it off – less than 600 souls in Washington. Assuming others will do the little deeds for you to protect your future for you is the most dangerous way to think for the large majority. The answer is little, easy-to-do details which are easy to repeat. These deeds work to unite the majority to regain power. MOMENTUM IS THE KEY!

The Great Majority Power Move puts an end to big money exploitation and big money campaigns with a real voice from the majority. Use this majority power-move to change direction from the worst power-grab by the few trying to lead us in their direction. Currently, while our military might is being stretched into submission by an over-extended war and billions more to spend, China is quietly building its military might. At current pace, China's military power will eventually look like Goliath next to ours. The few won't talk about this so it is up to the majority to speak!

The few are foolishly exploiting the majority. In doing so, they are weakening America's power base and transferring the great power to communist China leaders. That throws balance of power way off balance and makes America vulnerable to the worst power grab of all led by communist China leaders who want nothing more than to own America's resources. To America's human treasures, communist leaders find you replaceable and all who love freedom are liabilities. Their population of 1.3 billion and their system of skimming all of the profits at the top while their nation lives in poverty is dangerous to America's human treasures. Choose to support a new direction, or by default, you will support the current direction giving power to China. If we don't do the same thing together to change direction, their policies will beat us into enslavement with their low price first. That would happen before we see their military guns. Even if that were to happen in twenty to forty years, anytime is too soon! Why keep supporting that direction? As Americans, we need the brightest ways to think running deep within our veins, ways which raise the greatest nation in every prosperous way opposite to every failure and great expense. Change happens by repeating The Great Majority Power Move. This book and www.USAFreedom.us provide the details.

P.S. – Repeating the Great Majority Power Move is the answer. Each telling ten others for nine days will reach 300 million in nine days. For each to wait one month to talk with one, we wouldn't do it in five years. Then, we'd be up to our eye-balls in communist economics and deepening poverty. Children would take the hit for our indifference.

Why The Great Majority Power Move Is Needed

Without any fault of the majority, today's media dominates the airwaves with convenience and the public finds it a true convenience. Unfortunately, this same convenience fails to represent the majority politically because most of it is paid for by big money. The majority has no political voice. This is why the Great Majority Power Move is needed. The best way to achieve new direction is to gain powerful new majority voice. Change the elections system so leaders from the majority are elected rather than big money. This is how to return to a representative form of government and a people's state rather than a corporate state mindlessly transferring the power to communist China's military state.

A campaign to win back an honest and fair election system must come from the majority. It won't happen by big money advertising working opposite. A campaign coming from the simple efforts of the majority is one that cannot be bought by big money. When the majority has compelling purpose right for them and opposite to communist economics coming from politicians in Washington, they don't need big money campaigns from politicians who offer more of the same. A simple, well-designed, low-cost grass roots campaign is all that is needed. The Great Majority Power Move is that plan. The majority of 300 million have all of the power over less than 600 souls in Washington. This is the message worth repeating in great majority numbers. This Great Majority Power Move is the way to repeat it for great majority change. It happens by goodness within us and the power of one combined voice over the few in Washington by repeating the message.

P.S. – See at the END of this book the Petition for America. It demands the replacement of big money campaigns with publicly funded debates. Majority strength can end corruption in government! See more at: www.USAFreedom.us

Gain critical new direction and end corruption with a new election system not paid for by big money. Have fun with the great majority power move. Join with others from the 300 million-majority for the best system of change. Change happens by repeating the simple parts of the Great Majority Power Move!

How The Great Majority Power Move Works

300 million voices outnumber 536 failed politicians by over 500,000 to one! See below how the message will spread even more through all major media - talk radio, news print, T.V., and internet to overwhelm 536 failed politicians. The voice of 300 million is easy to repeat and overwhelming in power! Repeat the littlest deeds below by millions to do the largest good! Immediate response will build momentum FAST!

1. Tell ten others as soon as possible about this book, the website www.USAFreedom.us, and this grassroots campaign for ending corruption in government! Do it FAST and gain momentum FAST with many doing this! Each telling ten others will spread it FAST!

2. Email favorite pages from the USAFreedom.us website to others with the touch of a "send key!"

Email best-read topics to family, friend, neighbor, newspaper editor, TV talk show host, spiritual leader, and/or community, and/or government leaders! Feel free to copy and paste content from this website to do so.

3. Purchase the "Fashion of Freedom" shirt on the USAFreedom.us website. It will do more for you than any other shirt! It advertises the USAFreedom.us website and most empowering insights to hundreds, thousands, and millions who view it. Also enjoy most exceptional conversations by wearing it. Wear this shirt to improve opportunity for one and all for the best future possible opposite to the worst path we are on now led by communist economics. Nothing could mean more to your future than "Freedom"!

Since you've got to wear a shirt anyway, it might as well be "Freedom"! Other shirts have no message and no solution. Fashions of Freedom offer America's most attractive colors and America's best value in apparel. It's really about your entire future. Other apparel has no message and no future!

Shirt buyers also receive FREE MEMBERSHIP to Team USA along with Team USA e-news, progress reports, and opportunity to participate in coordinated national efforts to achieve REAL change.

Individuals, retail stores, and small business of ALL types can retail this shirt for profit while also building the majority voice for change.

4. Purchase more copies of "Returning to America", and share it with others - the book that will change America!

5. Get "Petition for America" signatures (found at the END of this book). This will also introduce others to the mission, the USA Freedom website, and the Great Majority Power Move. Doing this will have huge impact!

6. Do the Walk for America to gain public notice of this effort. See the details in an up-coming section.

7. All major media will be used for making this most public.

P.S. – The Great Majority Power Move gives 300 million the choice to be quiet like mice or opinionated like men. The one choice is slavery. The other is USA freedom!

P.P.S. – The more 300 million repeat the Great Majority Power Move, the more power there is to restore the nation of our dreams. Idle response supports current direction and is self-destructive to all you desire! Some will not lift a finger to improve the future for freedom's children. Enough others can make a difference. Don't let the future go to slavery! Together, we CAN change course!

Team USA

All great success happens ON A TEAM. This is the best way for America to win for THE BEST FUTURE! This is also the only viable way to change direction.

TEAM USA is the team for those Americans who want the power of teamwork along with deep and powerful reform. The odds are 300 million with the compounding power of teamwork to 536 failed politicians. It happens when America's majority join forces as one to stop the sale of the people's state to a corporate state, political state, foreign state, and communist state by the elite few. TEAM USA is the means to work together with many human parts working as one!

Teamwork is absolutely required for deep and powerful reform. This is the same way a super bowl team wins. A player joins the team in August with accumulated talent far beyond his own. The team grows in skill, power, and effectiveness many months until February. Then, after MANY smaller wins, the entire team through accumulated STRENGTH wins the super bowl. All great wins happen this way.

There must be organized effort to win America's game FOR THE BEST FUTURE! TEAM USA is the answer to take back America!

MEMBERSHIP IS FREE and can be displayed for all to see by simply wearing ANY FASHION OF FREEDOM SHIRT available for purchase on the USA Freedom website. Such visual display is essential!

MEMBERSHIP to Team USA INCLUDES free Team USA e-news, progress reports, and opportunity to participate in coordinated national efforts to achieve REAL change!

Fashion of Freedom shirts and free membership sign-up are available at www.USAFreedom.us. To receive free email updates and progress reports by e-news, subscribe to FREE E-NEWS SUBSCRIPTION on the shirts page. This is also how to receive FREE MEMBERSHIP.

Twelve Questions And Answers That Matter Most To All Americans

1. How can you know where your future in your country is headed? Those who know the trends can also know the future. Simply look at current trends, how they develop, and imagine what they will look like at full maturity. The answer will tell you what the future holds. America is currently headed for its worst nightmare - a full-blown course in communist economics taking shape in a way certain to cause the worst poverty conditions economically, politically, spiritually, and in every way in ripple effect. There is ample reason to believe that current conditions will be grossly worse if present trends continue.

2. Why should America change direction? Current direction is leading America down a path just like every path has a sequence of steps which continues in one progressive direction. The longer we continue this way, the worse it gets. The path includes a partnership with China and influence by communist China. Even the smallest brain would have to acknowledge that China's influence on America's way of life is growing steadily day-by-day. China's economic grip is around America's throat and America needs the character to remove it! China's path by sheer speed and size is progressing to a state of unprecedented global power. In very short time, at current growth rate, China will be far more powerful than America as a super power, and with unprecedented influence. This path has many more steps and more progress certain to lead America to the worst outcomes with communist economics as our guide and everything that flows with their economics – their economic policy, their political policy, and their religious policy which dictates our religious policy and all else that China implements regularly on China's path. This situation is far more serious than most have considered and this is reason for change!

3. Why should America's majority hold politicians accountable for their voting records? Presently, politicians are using a "cloak of secrecy" behind closed doors. They know they can vote on issues good for their political careers but not good for public policy. They are not being held

personally accountable. They know the general public is too busy to be watching. This gives them room to vote to serve their political careers more than public policy.

4. How can politicians be held accountable for their voting records? Corral them for the same reason livestock is corralled. Force their vote in a most public way so corruption is exposed and ended by the means to make it happen. Unless we do this, it won't happen on its own! This happens by making the Petition for America most public. The more public support this petition gets, the more effective it will be! Many signatures and The Great Majority Power Move is how to support it!

5. Why are term limits critical? Term limits limit incentive to repeat what politicians are repeating most now which is voting to preserve their careers and self interests. Term limits will also draw fresh perspective to the political arena with ideas and values needed most for dramatic change opposite to the status quo in Washington. Term limits will provide new political choices in Washington different from those stuck in office now.

6. Why should self-absorbing financial perks be removed from the pay of political servants? Self-absorbing perks work contrary to the interests of the public because they fail to give politicians right incentive to fix what needs fixing. Currently, politicians are doing nothing to fix problems because they don't have the same problems as the people being served. The social security fiasco is a good example of that. While the senate and congress have padded their pay plans with something much better, they are spending the public's retirement money in social security to pay for their political bills. This is stealing. This money doesn't belong to them!

7. What common sense solution is required to fix our current election system now? Anyone with the smallest brain, including politicians, would know that the two-party system is failing. This system must be eliminated to rid America of the two-party electoral system only favoring two failed parties. Expensive campaign financing buying the

election process must also go. Solution? End campaign support from the corrupt corporate system. Limit campaign contributions to the human majority and public tax revenues, not corporations! This way, the human majority representing the people's state will be served. Consider a maximum $100.00 contribution limit per individual contributor. The rest can come from public tax revenues to pay for public debates. This will end big-money contributions from large corporations.

8. What is the real situation with the two-party political system and why must this system be changed? The system of electing leaders to lead is the very means by which the future is shaped. This is paramount to the future of all Americans and this is why the election system must be fixed in order to elect right leaders to office. The two-party system has MANY restrictions and limitations for those with honest intent to run for office. By eliminating these restrictions and limitations, more qualified leaders will have the option to run for office and fill most vital roles of public service. Not one original U.S. president would have qualified to be a candidate based on today's unreal and corrupt election standards bought and paid for by big money. All of them would have been disqualified for lack of funds.

9. Why is it so important to be able to elect the right kind of president? The right kind of president will affect the future of all American's most more than any other just because this office is the highest in the land. Therefore, it is important to have right candidates to produce right outcomes. Our present system obviously fails to do that.

Top candidates are not likely to come from inside of the box of common failure. This is because they have already proven to be unfit to speak a message of change because they haven't done it. Just to give them the benefit of the doubt however, it would be fair to say that the right person, whether that be an incumbent politician or not, will speak a message far more potent then the problems we face. The answers will also make perfect sense as truth always makes perfect sense and much more sense than all happening now which is total failure.

10. How can you know for certain when a politician is speaking truth or a lie? When a politician is speaking truth, real problems are addressed as well as real solutions. When problems are not addressed, either out of ignorance or deception, solutions will not be addressed either. There can be no solution without an accurate acknowledgement of problems.

Truth is the answer to everything whether politicians know it or not. Truth is truth even if no one believes it. A lie happens when there is failure to recognize truth either by sheer ignorance or by intent. Regardless, you can always tell if a politician is lying if he or she fails to address real problems accurately and the opposite solutions on the other side.

11. Does the majority of 300 million have the voting power to override a small group of self-interests in Washington? Absolutely! It is 300 million compared to 536 in Washington.

12. Can the majority win the next presidential race even though big money is exploiting the minds and character of our politicians in Washington? The answer is yes! The answer is very simple and within easy grasp for 300 million. Simply look at the numbers in the question just above. They are overwhelming! Then look at my empowerment plan for the majority to reclaim the economic and political system from a small group leading America down the worst of paths led by big money exploitation and communist economics at its worst. The answers are simple. Response by those who read this will be the sum total of the response of the majority. The majority must rise in leadership to reclaim the future for all of freedom's children!

P.S. – Just as you wouldn't expect a super bowl team to win without a game plan, the same is true for America! America must have a game plan to win! This book details that plan!

P.P.S – Communist economics occurs when people earning $2.00 per day make consumer goods we buy. That would ruin you!

Our Politicians – Those Bastards

If many government leaders in Washington worked in any career other than politics, some would be fired for lack of intellect, lack of heart, lack of leadership, and lack of competence! Others would be tried as criminals!

Here is a list of indiscretions happening ON THEIR WATCH –

Transferring the people's state to a corporate state and a foreign state led by none other than communist China!

Selling off the people's interests to corporate interests for personal gain!

Allowing corporate executives to influence government policies and then practice economic abuse of the people's state!

Failing to govern government which is supposed to govern and protect the interests of the people. Instead, government is broken and ineffective because those in Washington lack intellect and leadership to govern!

Just as they have destroyed small family farms, they are now destroying small family business, family practice, family living, and family values! They are wiping out small business by giving the lion's share of benefit to large business bought and paid for by big money!

Will enough from the 300 million-majority end corruption by the few? Will they repeat the easy-to-repeat steps provided in the Great Majority Power Move? This would give them overwhelming power! Will they grab their power to head off the worst possible America nightmare?

The Great Majority Power Move makes necessary change simple! 300 million now have power to duplicate one voice to end corruption, change direction, and dramatically improve America! Nothing will improve your future more than improving the nation which makes up every part OF YOUR LIFE!

How To Hold Politicians Publicly Accountable

Promote the 2007 Petition for America! Force the vote of elected officials so each of them are exposed on the largest issues. Also, follow their voting records to make sure they are staying honest. Also, talk, talk, talk with others about this book and the USA Freedom website. Have others sign the Petition for America a.s.a.p.! Let's have millions of signatures by September 15, 2007 and millions more after that! Everyone doing a little will do a lot!

Can 300 Million Really Restore The Greatest Nation?

When 300 million repeat anything together, it is powerful! Especially so when the Great Majority Power Move is repeated! The Great Majority Power Move is just the response needed to transform America in most significant positive ways opposite to America's worst nightmare. All of the worst comes from bad economic policy like the policy we have now led by corporate exploitation by the few and communist economics. Please note that communist economics is so significant in size to have dramatic effect upon America unless we the people stop that from happening. Awakening one great majority to do so is far more important than electing one good president. Change can happen by awakening one great majority to repeat the Great Majority Power Move in unison. This move gives sweeping power to the majority to change the future for all Americans like nothing in public domain. This is the right answer!

Some think this kind of achievement is unachievable because they only look at what they've seen from 536 failed politicians in Washington. This is one president, 435 in congress, and 100 senators. These are the ones representing the current broken leadership system. Washington politicians simply have no answers, only failure. Don't judge our opportunity by their failure. The great majority hasn't heard one thing from Washington worth hearing because leaders at the top aren't even thinking about restoring the greatest nation. The best they can offer is a surface fix. This message is different! It is about restoring the greatest nation from the direction of deep poverty and failure coming from the progressive advancement of communist economics in America. Awaken the giant! The Great Majority Power Move is opposite to every failure and expense. It delivers the brightest solutions and most dramatic results on the other side.

For the majority, this is a goal worth pursuing – opposite to our worst nightmare!! I'd rather fight for change than to lie down and let corporate exploitation and communist economics roll all over us! The answer is opposite to the patterns of total failure that are happening now. Under the current plan, America's economic state will continue to sink in a way that most would find hard to imagine unless direction is changed. Also, because economic means is the means to all else, all else will become much worse based on current bad economic policy!

This message defines two ways and two choices – either greatest success or worst nightmare. The choice is yours by what you do. Greatest success happens by doing things right. Our greatest nightmare happens by remaining idle. The choice is simple for the 300 million-majority. The answers are also obvious. Continue as we are or change!

Can 300 million do it? Yes! It just requires enough response to repeat the message of the Great Majority Power Move! Many together can effect real change opposite to the worst nightmare. Any less response would be completely unthinkable since poor response would spell certain slavery.

The majority of 300 million have the compounding power of teamwork. The answer is so simple when the odds are 500,000 to every one politician. The majority can have anything they want with one voice together. Please note that some politicians are already on our side! Of course not all from the majority will respond. Only the smart ones will because they don't want to risk losing to this present system growing progressively worse. The goal is to reach enough of the smart ones to change direction.

Why A Power Grab By Communist China Has Real Potential

Quick comparisons show why! China's has the largest population of all and a much larger population of 1.3 billion compared to the U.S. population of 300 million. This population difference gives the few at the top of the communist party a much larger opportunity to skim profits for the few and gather more power. This also gives China a much larger opportunity to grow as a world power of the worst kind both economically and militarily. This is true while America's economic forecast is working in the opposite direction due to costly trends shaping our U.S. future – bulging health care costs, bulging military costs, and other large costs because of social, academic, economic, and spiritual decline.

Besides having to compete with China's low price, the global economy is forcing American workers and businesses to compete with every slave labor practice around the globe. Such slave practice is bad for the whole world. Our politicians are foolishly giving America's power to that system.

The government of communist China is a dangerous business player to compete with because China's business is also ruled directly by military strength held by the few with no checks and balances. As business power goes to China, so does military power!

From the above, it is easy to see why America will need far more intelligence than that in Washington responsible for all of the failure. Obviously, new direction is needed opposite to the current way generating large expense and failure. The U.S. Constitution, when properly observed, obviously provides many more checks and balances to protect human interests from the worst power grabbers compared to communism which offers no protection and no comparison.

P.S. – This book contains the only game plan in sight to save America from the worst to come. That is, the destructive power of communist economics. It is also the only game plan with power to save it.

The Walk For America

Draw attention to this purpose and make it most public. Momentum is absolutely required to revitalize America. Momentum is also easy to gain. It includes the Walk for America. The Walk for America is an excellent opportunity to draw attention to change. Walking events and public events all across America is an effective way to do it.

Carry banners, signs, and everything possible to promote the USA Freedom website and this book. This is YOUR campaign for YOUR future. Do it in parades, rallies, and wherever possible. It can happen on July 4th, "parade day" when all gather to celebrate Independence Day. It can also happen at other public events throughout the year. When people gather, take the opportunity to heighten public awareness. Even have rallies of your own.

Nothing speaks the message better than this book, the USA Freedom website, and the shirt for promoting the message. Wear your Fashions of Freedom to show America's most important message and the best freedom shirt in all of the land. You can also sell the shirt for profit at public events. For details, email from the USAFreedom.us website to learn how. Have as many people as possible join in the Walk for America to make a large public statement.

The same can also be accomplished on Memorial Day, Labor Day, and every other day in the year where events occur.

Please take every opportunity to promote this book, the USA Freedom website, and this mission to change America. Do it in convenient ways for love of country and continued freedom for all of freedom's children. The Great Majority Power Move makes it simple.

Also, circulate the Petition for America for signing and promotion.

The Petition for America is a public mandate for politicians to change direction for all of freedom's children. The petition is at the END of this book.

P.S. - Invite all who want new direction and a better future to join in the Walk for America and together we CAN make a difference for the future of all!

P.P.S. – Fashions of Freedom can be ordered at: www.USAFreedom.us

About Apathy, Indifference, And Defeat

Apathy, indifference, and defeat can destroy your quality of life and the nation of your dreams. This also includes the quality of life and dreams of your children and your children's children.

Where do apathy, indifference, and defeat come from? They come from looking to Washington for answers. The answers are in us. There can't be an energetic, caring, and successful government of the people when government of the people is being abused and economically raped by government officials. Government of the people was made to fix it. Good followers come from good leaders. Both are required in government of the people. Good leadership with a good message to awaken the giant can end apathy, indifference, and defeat.

This book is a good message with power to awaken the giant. Every American should own a copy of this book to practice being American. It is not American to have apathy, indifference, and defeat. All those who fail to love this country and take care of it, should leave.

P.S. – In up-coming pages, see more about replacing big-money campaigns and big-money corruption with publicly funded debates. This is how to elect good leaders, have good government, and end apathy, indifference, and defeat.

The following fifteen best-read articles can be sent to local and national newspapers and other public media for printing. Call the editorial manager of your favorite newspaper/s to request printing. These articles can be duplicated by whatever means you choose. The easiest is by copy and paste from the www.USAFreedom.us website and then, sent by email. Find these on the Answers Page of the USA Freedom website under "Press Release"!

Editorial One
The Great Majority Power Move

The Great Majority Power Move is the means for 300 million Americans to reclaim America the Beautiful for all of freedom's children. It is the message and means not one American had before. Now each of 300 million can. Not one had before a message and a comprehensive plan with power to change the nation. Not one had before a website, a book, and a game plan to do it. Not one had before a potent voice beyond big money advertising and 536 failed politicians to reclaim the nation of their dreams. For 300 million, no longer does it make sense to be without the message. Reclaim the nation of your dreams from America's worst nightmare. Welcome The Great Majority Power Move!

The Great Majority Power Move is a real grassroots campaign like none in recent time. No longer does it make sense to look to 536 failed politicians. The power is in "we the people!" 300 million repeating the same voice together can end the worst nightmare – the few selling the majority to corporate exploitation, communist economics, and the worst poverty to come. The details of this plan give 300 million-strong overwhelming power over 536 failed politicians. It happens by repeating the same great power move millions of times over to change direction. The results can be overwhelming simply by doing it together. This is the REAL way to change. The majority is the right group to change it. Politicians in Washington won't. They are already proven failures. This plan provides the means to do it with simple, easy-to-repeat ways for achieving the goal. The results are opposite to the poverty plan in place now leading America's work force to poverty with billions across the globe earning $2.00 per day. Under the current plan, ruthless exploitation, price gouging, deep poverty, and the worst nightmare will continue to change the face of America forever. The Great Majority Power Move is the answer. No other plan will reward you more and no other means more to your future!

End the current corrupt election system so the majority can elect leaders from the majority including a new president representing the majority. It happens with a great majority power move. Under the current election system, presidential choices are limited to the few stars of failure from two failed political parties. This is the few in Washington with millions of dollars to start. Once these softies get in, their loyalties go to big money interests that get them there. This is not representative form of government and government of the people as described in our U.S. Constitution. This failed system must end. For this reason, the presidential race I was considering, I have dropped for a more fundamental task – replacing the current broken election system!

The following is included in the Great Majority Power Move.

End corruption in government within one year. This can happen as soon as the majority takes the simple steps below to regain power. Sooner is better than later so we don't elect another incompetent president to lead us deeper into communist economics. We can't take four more years of the same. We must have the choice to elect leadership with intellect and courage to end communist economics!

Replace big money campaigns and big money corruption with publicly funded debates. This will give the majority presidential choices based on content rather than big pocket books.

Talk of treason for those in government who continue to sell off the people's sovereign state to a corporate state and a foreign state led by communist China.

Empower the majority with a promotion campaign operated by the majority for the majority so the majority of 300 million-strong have the means to reclaim America from the few selling it off – that is less than 600 souls in Washington. (Assuming others will do the little deeds for you to protect your future for you is the most dangerous way to think for the large majority. The answer is little, easy-to-do details the majority can find simple to do. These deeds work to unite the majority to regain power!) MOMENTUM IS THE KEY!

The Great Majority Power Move puts an end to big money exploitation and big money campaigns with a real voice from the majority. Use this majority power move to change direction from the worst of power-grabs by the few who are giving us that direction. Currently, while our military might is being stretched into submission by an over-extended war and billions more to spend, China is quietly building its military might. At current pace, China's military power will eventually look like Goliath next to ours. The few won't talk about this so it is up to the majority to speak!

The few are foolish for exploiting the majority. In doing so, they are weakening America's power base and transferring the great power to communist China leaders. That throws balance of power way off balance and makes America vulnerable to the worst power grab of all led by communist China leaders who want nothing more than to own America's resources. To America's human treasures, communist leaders find you replaceable and all who love freedom are liabilities. Their population of 1.3 billion and their system of skimming all of the profits at the top while their nation lives in poverty is dangerous to America's human treasures. Choose to support a new direction, or by default, you will support the current direction giving power to China! If we don't do the same thing together to change direction, their policies will beat us into enslavement with their low price first. That would happen before we see their military guns. Even if that were to happen in twenty to forty years, anytime is too soon! Why keep supporting that direction? America needs the brightest ways to think running deep within our veins, ways that raise the greatest nation in every prosperous way opposite to every failure and great expense! Change starts by repeating The Great Majority Power Move! This book and www.USAFreedom.us give the details.

Large response to the Great Majority Power Move is the most certain way to achieve most desired results! Be empowered! Overshoot the goal for the top way to reach the goal!

Editorial Two
End Big Money Campaigns & Corruption

The answer is simple! Replace big money campaigns with publicly funded debates. Currently, big money is buying our politicians and government and leading America from a people's state to a corporate state run by a small group of greedy elite. This paves the way for an easy power grab by communist China. Currently, big money trade policy with communist China is lowering the economic standards of America's power base, the middle class majority. This is happening while China is silently building its economic might and military might to look like Goliath next to ours. This also means the power grabbers in Washington are foolishly transferring America's power base to communist China!

Big money is running our country and our election system now and it is time to end that practice. Find out whom each one of them supports, communist China's rule and the small group of big money power grabbers, or America's human treasures and the land of the free!

The easy way to end the corrupt political system immediately and end corruption in Washington is to end the big money election system bought and paid for by big money! Demand that your senator and congressman in Washington pass legislation in 2007 to replace big money campaigns with publicly funded debates so there can be a real presidential election in 2008.

The last time Senators McCain and Feingold accomplished campaign finance reform it was a joke thanks to the elite few in Washington giving us communist economics and corruption in government.

Do the above within one year with a great majority power move. Do this or idle response will reap America's worst nightmare. See more at: www.USAFreedom.us.

Editorial Three
Time For Change

America's population of 300 million is competing with billions of impoverished workers across the globe from China, India, Pakistan, and more. The common similarity in these three (all have populations of one billion or more) is that all three have a small population of the wealthy at the top and all of the rest poor. You may have seen the CNN News Reports that India's population has eighty percent of its work force earning $2.00 per day. Our politicians see no problem competing with such bottom heavy populations of poor people.

If the people of America don't take appropriate action and demand a nationally managed economy with control of greed from within America's borders, all of Mexico's population and all of America's population combined would not be near enough to compete with billions of poor workers across the globe.

If we don't manage greed from within and show the world how to manage a balanced economy where all are working and making decent wages, how could we expect another like communist China to do it for us?

Anyone with intellect will also have intellect to know where America is headed. Currently not one president, congressman, or senator is showing the intellect to recognize this.

Our safety net is our U.S. Constitution. It calls for government of the people. Our people of 300 million far outnumber our president, congressmen, and senators when we gather as one in unified strength. Let's tell them what we want! If we don't want to lose what we have and see our children working for the same wages as those in this large "out of control" global economy, we the people must insist on a new direction. If we don't, America the beautiful will be a thing of the past.

Our president, congress, and senate are all following and not leading. They are showing they know nothing about managing an economy. They are following the lead of communist China with a population of 1.3 billion. This is why some of them say we need Mexico's illegal immigrant population and their cheap labor for our economy. If we continue to allow such thinking, this need won't stop until our nation looks like China and India. Don't our government leaders know anything about direction? Does it make any sense to you why America's population of 300 million should be competing with billions of economically impoverished people from China, Pakistan, and India? This is incentive for us to stand together and change direction of our country.

To take back America, go to: www.USAFreedom.us.

P.S. - No longer does democrat or republican mean anything! Both have made themselves irrelevant. The only two political parties remaining are those who vote to favor the few (including communist economics) and the other – those who support the people's state, government of the people! Promote the difference between these two and you will divide out and conquer those favoring the few!

Editorial Four
Root Of All Solutions

When love of money is the root of all evil, managing greed is the root of all solutions.

Some think a market-driven economy led by those who hold the power of money is the only factor needed for managing an economy. They are naïve to the power of greed. Greed is a self-consuming sickness with most destructive power. It also needs to be managed.

You would keep the wolf out of the back yard where your children play wouldn't you?

America faces something never seen before - a corporate system of global greed that is uncontrollable in the way business is presently done. If this course is continued, the whole world is likely to follow and be managed by the greatest evil, then, all would be subjects of it.

World-class poverty comes from world-class greed. Most economic problems today, large and small, stem from this global system of greed – the root of all evil. Rather than economic fighting within, we should be working together to rebuild our national economy opposite to global greed. America's borders can and should be protected. This includes protection from the world's lowest poverty standards and the greatest evil.

America's economy currently is being led by the low price of China. China's population of 1.3 billion is much larger than ours of 300 million. Also, their system skims the profits and the power for the few at the top while they exploit their own at poverty wages. There are no checks and balances in their system. Our country is becoming more and more like theirs by competing with them and billions of impoverished workers across the globe. Our elected leaders are foolishly taking us to the lowest poverty standards.

The golden rule is the time-proven prosperity plan for every nation – Treat others how you would like to be treated. A counterfeit golden rule also exists which looks good from the surface but leads to human failure and poverty in the long run. It teaches, "He who has the gold has the rule!" All nations living by the counterfeit rule have only two classes, the few at the top and all the rest poor - a most unsightly sight! America is on that path and if continued, will find itself at a point of no return in a large out of control global economy led by only a few at the top who are most evil. At that point, most Americans would be subjects of that evil. Even those with wealth would lose to the wicked.

If we don't want that to happen, we must govern and manage greed at our borders and within our borders. This can happen by government of the people and proper government regulation by taxing greed to remove incentive.

Remove incentive that is destructive to harmonious business and harmony among neighbors. Eliminate practices improperly exploiting the good. Embrace much higher economic standards to improve our economy from the inside out and bring balance back to trade so all work together as friends and neighbors in one successful economy. We are a nation of plenty if we treat others as we would like to be treated.

Our best option now is aggressive action to protect the future for all of freedom's children. This includes working together as one majority to elect the right president with a game plan true to sound principle. This is something Washington politicians haven't done. China is already in position to lead. If we continue in apathy and indifference, we will eventually be managed like livestock for lack of responsibility.

A system run by the world's largest players of greed is the largest threat to our future. This is a very real threat with power to reduce many to poverty and set off many other events of failure but not if we stand together to change it. Our future requires a president and government leaders who can re-install sound business to our economy. Politicians have already proven they know nothing about business. Corporate thugs won't do. A new election system can produce the right kind of leaders with the skill and aptitude like nothing we've seen in Washington. This is also the way to benefit small business, family business, family values, and human values. This is how to re-establish freedom's rule. For success far beyond any put into words by any recent president, go to: www.USAFreedom.us.

Editorial Five
How To Improve Education

Our president wants to improve our education system so our children can compete better in the global economy? How about telling him to improve the foundation of education so education can improve. The foundation of education is the family environment of security and love for children. This happens in an economic environment where the needs of families and family life are protected through sound economic policy. How can children be great students if they don't feel secure and loved?

Because our economy is competing with every impoverished child-labor state across the globe, our economy and our education policy for children are both suffering. Why should our kids compete with them anyway? Their children work like slaves, act like wards of state, and have no beliefs of their own! Kids greatest education comes from having two happy-in-love parents at home, living and playing together as family, livelihood of family, and sound economic policy for supporting all of the above.

Remember how our education system began? It began with the best prosperity system of all, the family unit and small family business. Children lived with, played with, and worked with their parents on the family farm or small family business. The family unit was a self-contained prosperity system. This was also the finest education institution on earth. As early as five years old, children learned to do little chores for dad and mom. As they grew, they learned how to work physically and physical work taught them how to work mentally. Work gave them self-identify, self-respect, and self-dignity. This was a solid base for learning. Children also had successful relationships with family in the family business and they watched how their parents had successful relationships with others through the same. Their parents also applied the golden rule. They treated others in business how they wanted to be treated. The golden rule taught children the most valuable lessons about themselves and others and how to prosper in most rewarding ways. This was our country's prosperity system and it prospered our economy. As a result, there was also economic equality among those who worked. Children also learned the skills of carrying on the family livelihood or business.

How about going for a re-designed economy once again which serves the land of the free! It models the golden standards it was built on. We know this one much better than communism. This is also a model for the rest of the world to follow rather than follow the lead of communist rule where China dominates through economic, political, and military power. Through legislation and tax practice, our national leaders can take every opportunity and every step to favor small business, family business, and the golden rule which guides them. Isn't it time for a political and economic over-haul? Surface change will not do. We have the opportunity to replace the abuse of a small minority so the large majority can enjoy prosperity the way they should based on the most tried and true traditional values and not communist economics!

How about demanding from one president, congress, and senate an improved national educational policy by protecting those elements which contribute most to it. Protect our economy, livelihoods, small business, and family business from abusive power. When children see how leaders take care of them, they will know how to take care of others including their children later in life. This is how to improve education and benefit our children and our nation's future most.

We need success put into words like no politician has. For answers beyond politics, go to: www.USAFreedom.us

Editorial Six
Revitalize America

Nothing could be more anti-Christ and opposite to the will of the people than the global corporate system led by communist economics. But then, you already knew this! Those with the eagle's view know America needs a total fix rather than a surface fix. One more president lacking depth to fix the system would put us into mortgage beyond belief to China. So far no politician has even come close to addressing the problem. This must happen before a solution is gained. (We'd be foolish to believe any politician who wasn't first straight about our problems.) The answer comes from going opposite to failure with saving grace for self, family, and country.

Since livelihood is the lion's share of life, small business and family business are top priority. These are good for the family, business, and economy. They also work opposite to the global corporate system. They enhance relationships at every level providing the necessary teamwork to work together to revitalize and rebuild our economy. They also employ the smartest of all business rules - treat others as you would want to be treated. This golden rule empowers us to prosper our selves by prospering others. This rule also works to prosper our entire economy. This model is salvation to our way of life and economy. Currently our lawmakers are ignorantly walking all over it with their ignorant laws. We need a whole nation inspired to do something remarkable - remake America free from communist rule! We must think and act better if we want to keep our way of life from communist economics and their rule. Change requires a new model. If we don't make this change, America's worst nightmare will be our result for failure to act!

Replace the rule that says, "He who has the gold has the rule!" This rule gives the economic power to the most unsavory. It benefits the selfish few and causes the rest to be poor. This rule would eventually put most of the power in the hands of the most wicked. Most of the money right now is going to China led by communist economics. If the wicked were to rule the world, even they could learn they wouldn't be happy with the world they rule. All of life is better by making life better for others. Teamwork on a local, national, and global scale is what we need to keep our standards.

We can't afford another average president. We need outstanding answers in someone who can lead the choice between the best and the worst and give the clearest choice between the two because there are only two. The worst is communist economics in America and communist rule. Those who have the gold have the rule. The best is power over it by restructuring our way back to the right rule and sound economics. We need a successful model for energizing all Americans, democrats, republicans, and all of us together! Pursue only one new direction with whole heart and unrelenting resolve! The one rule produces everything we could want. The other loses it to communist economics. There are always answers on the other side of failure and for every evil there is much greater good on the opposite side. We need tried and true traditional ways which favor America and not communist rule. We need the best of humanity spread across the globe. We need the home, family, family living, family practice, family values, family business, and all of humanity together in the right economic model. None can do it better than small business, family business, and the golden rule to guide us. We can't have values in America again unless we return to this. The future requires it. By God's insight, we can change America for the better. Of course there are doubters and cynics who say it can't be done. Unbelievers won't do it. Don't let doubting tom only offer you the worst direction!

Let's be our own best leaders to get what we want. Let's talk solutions with others to awaken the giant. Washington won't listen until we awaken the giant. Please check out the Great Majority Power Move at: www.USAFreedom.us. This easy-to-do campaign is the only practical answer for awakening the giant!

Editorial Seven
Iraq War Strategy

Win The War In Iraq With Foolproof Basics

If there is one single most important way to win the war in Iraq, winning the war of ideas is number ONE! Obviously, the answer is not the current plan; generals, military might, or West Point doctrine. This plan is already proven not to be working. Right motivation is the answer and it happens with foolproof basics!

It happens by winning hearts and minds and knowing how success is made there.

Success is made with steps in the mind. This can also be called the path to greatest victory. This path matters most, more than a physical path, and more than military might because it shows how to accomplish every desire step by step. Most important are the steps in the mind with similar lessons to those on a physical path. The steps in the mind teach the series of steps, order of the steps, direction, effectiveness, timing, rhythm, momentum, progress, and everything needed to place us where we want to be.

The path in the mind is easiest of all to do and adjust for highest human performance – exactly the answer for winning hearts and minds in Iraq!

By the way, top brass in Washington might think this lesson is too simple for winning the war. I say, is it too low for their intelligence or does this very basic knowledge show their intellect is too low to grasp it? The best happens with rock-solid basics!

I believe the key to winning the war in Iraq is mostly about winning hearts and minds. This comes from motivation expertise, not military might or West Point doctrine.

Obviously, the path in the mind has all of the answers for placing us where we want to be including winning the war of ideas!

For more on winning the war of ideas, go to: www.USAFreedom.us and www.LifeStylersUSA.com.

Editorial Eight
Win Over Terror

Win the war on terror through bright thoughts more than military might and large costs. This is how and I think you'll agree.

For every evil there is an opposite good on the opposite side and a most effective answer in verbal form. It happens with a most compelling message on the other side of evil with logic for warming the world and showing the ignorance of terror too!

Give terrorists the personal image they want most to avoid. The most successful campaign will do that and do the best job to counter their campaign of terror. Image building is a universal human language, even to terrorists! Read on for more on image building for terrorists.

Part comes from promoting the right image for them. The other part comes from building the right image on the opposite side.

Warm the world by showing the good on the other side of evil. The brightest answers are opposite to the darkest evil. This is the brightest solution. This message isn't just for certain people of certain nations so it fits every person of every nation. The free world looks to the U.S. for all of it and especially from our leaders. Our leaders can speak to every heart about the good on the other side of terror. This is the message with power to win hearts and minds most effectively and far more effectively than bombs and guns. Save our military might, billions of dollars, and save our troops by winning the war with words! This is not to discount the other but words are much greater!

The high ways on the one side reveal how low the low ways are on the other side. Show how terror is a low-life school in the greatest ignorance and failure by showing the greater. There are many ways to say it and since no one wants to look stupid, what could be greater than to show terrorists how to avoid looking stupid by stopping the stupid acts they do! I also suggest we rename terrorists. No sense in giving them a name we don't like and one that feeds their ego. How about calling them nerds, uneducated, and everything rhyming with stupid. Nerd stands for "needs education real desperately".

Their ignorance has gained too much ground on the other side of good for lack of a proper message. I have heard much about the physical war but nothing of value for winning the war of ideas. The best offers the highest good to all, even to uneducated terrorists. Make the message most compelling and even some of them might even be won by the greatest good on the other side. When terrorism is about religion, tell the world that the best religions don't have to kill to win converts. That's weak and ignorant! The best give freedom to compare for the brightest answers. The best work by love and freedom of will, not by dictators, murderers, and other forms of evil.

The best anti-terror message I know has already been completed over two thousand years ago. It comes from the world's most influential leader, the world savior who taught how to negotiate with the devil and win, how to shut the mouth of lions and accusers, how to speak a message which changes the world, and how to live the ultimate dreams by going opposite to every failure! I'm applying for the job to do that in Washington and show government officials how. This also includes making heads of the terrorist movement accountable for their ignorance through much superior logic on the other side which loses appeal and following for dummies. After all, who wants to follow a dummy so give terrorists the image right for them! Expose the greatest evil and empower with the greatest good. Marketing the right message is precisely the best answer.

What could be greater than the message which shows every heart the greatest care, warmest embrace, and greatest answers! This message most public is the message most effective in winning over terror. Terrorists are ignorant of the greatest good. As a result, they sow evil and every form of failure. You can know them by their works. Love is the greatest on the opposite side. It sows tolerance of others, love for others, teamwork, prosperity, freedom of religion, and wholeness for individual and family. What could be greater?

If you like my message and want it said much more in Washington, support it - for anti-terror and all of your future! Support comes from buying my book, *Returning to America*, as well as the message shirt promoting the message. It also happens with the www.USAFreedom.us website which tells the message! Doing nothing helps the opposite message on the other side.

The "Freedom shirt" can be ordered on-line at: www.USAFreedom.us.

Spread the message about freedom and win over terror!

Editorial Nine
Policy On Global Economy

Policy on global economy starts with having a successful national economy, one which serves humanity within national borders. Marriage, family, children, livelihood, and national economy are all important.

When a nation knows how to care for its own, that nation can contribute to the global economy. A successful global economy happens when a world of nations shows responsibility to take care of their own.

Our most valuable export in America can be our knowledge and care to take care of our own and show other nations how. This way, we can spread freedom and not slavery around the globe.

Make national governments around the world accountable to serve their own people or show their people the right to remake government.

This global policy will give proper incentive to nations to be friendly to one another and work in harmony instead of war so all can work together to serve the needs of nations.

End entitlement thinking around the globe by making each national government accountable to serve its own or face consequence by the will of their people.

Teach the world the right of the people to have government of the people, by the people, and for the people or exercise their right to replace those in government giving the people slavery.

Empower the people to shape their will and you will have a better globe!

I support having good global partners who operate according to principles of truth and freedom. In the spirit of friendship, I support helping those who are willing to help themselves to live by truthful standards. Those who have no will should just plan on living in slavery. Let each nation be shaped by the will and judgment of its people.

I support helping as many nations as possible when we can to help further freedom, but first, we must take care of our own so we can model freedom for the world and not go broke in the process.

I support teaching how to fish rather than giving all of the fish away.

This is the policy I support on global economy.

For this and more for improving America, go to:
www.USAFreedom.us

Editorial Ten
Immigration Laws

America's immigration laws are served best by being true to the fundamentals of fair business where each party benefits fairly in business and there is fair trade at every level of trade. Exploitation is bad business because it tips the scale off balance. Exploitation produces absolute forms of slavery, economic and otherwise.

America's economy is like a bicycle. It will either have balance or fall. It must also support the needs of the middle-class majority or it will fall. It needs to be managed responsibly to do that. Leaders must know the difference between good and evil and how to manage with good.

I support an immigration policy which eliminates corruption and parasitic behavior from our government and business including illegal immigration and illegal exploitation of the disadvantaged. I support cleaning up business practice and reinstating ethics over exploitation so America can remain free.

I support the right to change the economic path of America so America doesn't continue on the path of communist economics. This path has power to reduce a whole nation to poverty just like the poor people have in China.

The best way to further freedom is to go with answers like these here.

I support a whole economy built on principles of wholeness where one and all can live together as neighbors and each can love the beautiful view they see in their next-door neighbor rather than the other view that all are slaves.

I support balancing business and economics at the same time where value is exchanged for value and all like working for a living. The other option is to continue down the current path. This is the path of communist China economics which will lead America to economic slavery just like the poor people of China. This is due to exploitation by the rich who live by greedy existence.

I support America's standard of one nation, under God, indivisible, with liberty and justice for all - for all nations because He teaches best how to live by love and not greed!

For neighbors from other countries wanting to enjoy America's freedom, they can by instituting "one nation, under God, indivisible, with liberty, and justice for all!"

I support a wall to protect our borders and the boarders of Mexico so character can rule in both America and Mexico. Then, both can live in freedom. We can also live together as close friends based on high performance human values. Then and only then, each can exchange value for value and be true friends.

This is where I stand on immigration laws - a standard within our borders for modeling true freedom for the rest of the world!

Grab your power to close our borders! See the power at: www.USAFreedom.us

P.S. – Tell the people of Mexico to end slave labor in Mexico so they don't bring slavery to America and contaminate America with the same human failure they need to fix in Mexico!

Editorial Eleven
The Model For Remaking The Economy

The model for remaking America's economy is simple and fair. Simple and fair is good perspective and the best perspective to apply to ALL economics for good economics.

America's best economy starts locally as oppose to globally. It starts with small business and enterprise of the human spirit with everyone working rather than global commerce and that big global super store! This way, everyone can have jobs and help each other. A great economy starts the way America started with small business. America can favor small business again through sound and easy to implement tax practice and proper legislation. It simply requires right leadership to do so. (See changing the election system with publicly funded debates.)

Local economies can first serve the locals while maximizing strength to serve other locals nationally. I support tapping the abundant resources of America to do it. America has abundance.

I support fair trade practices and federal regulation to bring local and national economies back into balance so we can continue to have a country. The goal is to reach a sustainable pricing structure so everyone can afford to trade with each other and still have jobs and profit in business.

Simple models are the answer to fair pricing.

The locals exchange what they have. Exchange bread for chicken, and chicken for beef so at the end of the day, everyone has what they need. America's economy is much more complex than that but fair pricing is America's economic solution. It comes from thinking simple and fair.

In addition, I support tax policies which serve small business. Small business is needed to bring jobs, balance, and success back to our economy.

I support real freedom versus economic slavery. This comes from addressing real problems at the roots to grow an economy on sound principles. If we do this, we will save our nation from living like the poor people of China.

This is the model for remaking the economy.

For most remarkable details for remaking America, go to: www.USAFreedom.us

Editorial Twelve
Smart Taxing

Smart is keeping taxing simple and manageable. Smart taxing is as simple as pie. It divides to your liking with the cut of a knife!

How is the pie cut presently? The few and the rich are getting richer for no profit to anyone. Greed makes them spiritually poor while all others grow poor financially. This is causing family, family values, and human values to plunder in America and around the world. I support another way!

Smart taxing can craft a way of life which serves human values and brings it back starting with marriage, family, and children.

Human values are America's real assets, not corporate structures, and the best comes from marriage, family, and children.

The higher purpose for business is serving people, not make slaves of them!

It doesn't happen by competing with China and China's human slave labor state like America is presently doing!

America's children and their families are taking the hit from our current economic policy competing with the worst human exploitation. Our leaders have shown no intellect to recognize this, much less manage it through smart taxation.

Things can turn around just by cutting the pie with the same kind of a precision as a surgeon with his knife, just as you wish.

Right now, America's economic policy is prospering the few at the top and even they are not happy in their self-absorbing greed.

Keep people first and you will have a very blessed country.

Let's improve our economic policy by helping people to be happy and prosperous without being unnecessarily rich with greed and empty purpose!

As top executives might put it, "I may not get filthy rich in America but is sure is nice to live in a nation where human values are number one!"

Too much fat at the top isn't doing any good.

Smart taxing can reshape America so quality of life returns. Smart taxing can also remove the incentive from greed.

Without humanity to sustain a country, there is nothing left of value!
If you want to put my message into practice, you can start by promoting this message for fixing America with answers for achieving most remarkable reform.

Buy the Fashion of Freedom shirt, share my book, *Returning to America*, with others, and email people in large numbers from the USA Freedom .us website. Remember to reach people of large influence, business leaders, ministers, politicians, and more. Send the book as a gift.

Smart taxing includes a whole economic policy for a blessed nation.

I support tax policies which remove incentive from greed. I support tax policies which favor those who work and contribute to economy and society. This includes right treatment of business too so all have major roles in winning!

There's prosperity again in America with smart taxing and a unified majority voice! It requires big change and big rewards for changing it! For how to do it, go to: www.USAFreedom.us

Editorial Thirteen
Equality Economics vs. Trash And Burn

The message is about our option as Americans to return to the most traditional and proven economic policy. I call it "equality economics". There is another option too which is to keep the present plan in place which is "trash and burn".

Your choice is to either continue supporting the ways of trash and burn or do something smart to return to equality economics in as many ways as possible! Trash and burn destroys! Equality economics makes whole!

Equality economics is a standard found in the Bible. This is how every successful economy works.

But by an equality, that now at this time your abundance may be a supply for their want, that their abundance also may be a supply for your want: that there may be equality:

Equality economics prospers all parties fairly in economic relationship and brings economic legitimacy to all parts of business.

Trash and burn mainly benefits certain parts with disproportionate advantage while other parts are trashed and burned. The bad thing about trash and burn is it's not sustainable to your future, and when given enough time, trash and burn will destroy your country!

America is at a point where trash and burn is no longer acceptable. For this reason, I support equality economics so America can have balance, success, and freedom back in our economy.

I support fair trade practices so all trades can prosper and have quality of life.

I support federal regulation and leadership oversight to bring balance back to America's pricing and trade practices so America can be one nation under God, indivisible, with liberty, and justice for all!

I support equality economics versus trash and burn!

To support equality economics, go to www.USAFreedom.us

P.S. – Americans are going to have to speak in plain English with family, friend, and neighbor about what is really going on in America regarding USA Freedom!

Editorial Fourteen
Government Of The People – Part One

Government of the people, by the people, and for the people is a basic provision of the U.S. Constitution. This message shows how simple and powerful this provision is and why it offers to one and all the most potent lessons of human empowerment!

Government of the people is the provision which gives to the people the ultimate human experience. This is practice in leadership to make life and government everything the people want it to be.

Government is a reflection of the people's desires, values, and choices.

The people have the power to shape government into everything they want it to be by a simple and powerful principle of "we the people". In America, a population of 300 million people working together far out-numbers a small number of senators, those in congress, and one president.

We the people must not think we are a small minority with little influence because in reality, we are a large majority of 300 million. We out-number the small group of less than six hundred in Washington by a large margin. The ratio is greater than 500,000 to every one politician.

The people represent a giant number and all of the people gathered together represent a huge majority of political power. This is the power of the great majority to act as one to take government of the people back. The formula is simple and so is the plan. The purpose for government of the people is freedom over slavery. There couldn't be a more important purpose for winning. Considering the alternative, anything less would be downright foolish!

Government of the people offers two courses of learning. One is best-case scenario of freedom which includes love for neighbor, jobs with fair wages, having fun through teamwork, and enjoying a rich social life of we the people! The other course is worst-case scenario. As one fellow businessperson said it, "If current direction continues, China will own America in twenty years lock, stock, and barrel!"

Many already know that a corporate take over of America is happening right before our eyes by the low price of China and communist rule. Our president speaks of protection like it is a bad word. He doesn't know anything smart! He said in his State of the Union address that America's economy is better with (illegal) migrant workers (which is slave labor). With his direction, much more slave labor will be needed!

Unlike our president, I believe protecting our country from evil is a good idea! Our president is mismanaging fairness and equality and trading it for slave labor. He also doesn't know how to manage fair trade and he can't with China's low price.

Why should America give up personal freedoms, fair trade, freedom of speech, freedom of religion, and much more for slave labor and the low price of China?

If the President doesn't already know it, communist economics is already in position to rule the world with China's low price and human slavery unless America changes direction through unified effort.

Should you want a winning game plan to reform the greatest nation, see The Great Majority Power Move on-line at: www.USAFreedom.us

P.S. - Let's show freedom's children how we support change for the good of all. Support to communist rule happens by idle response.

Editorial Fifteen
Iraq War Funding

George Bush wants more funding for Iraq.

Why trust him more to restore Iraq when he has failed to restore his own country? He has broken public trust because he has failed America's majority right at home!

How can there be anything good for America when America's military might is spent down to nothing in Iraq?

America's first line of defense happens at home! America must end communist economics in America or face the worse nightmare to come by competing with billions of workers across the globe earning $2.00 per day! America must throw out the book on the global economy and return to traditional values. These are the REAL values that are the timeless values for every nation!

Make no mistake! America the beautiful can longer continue business with every slave labor state across the globe and communist China economics! Already, many municipal and state governments are running broke! Already, government in Washington is looking more like government in Mexico with all of its corruption. More government leaders are on the take just like their Mexican counterparts. Also, more local, state, and federal governments are preying on the public with excessive fines and fees to raise revenue for THEIR broken governments!

Why put up with it any longer? I'd rather fight than lie down and let communist economics roll all over our nation! We can have much better if the majority repeats the same simple steps together to gain overwhelming power over less than 600 hundred souls in Washington. Should you want to stop the sale of your soul, you can. Don't allow ignorant, uncaring politicians sell your soul and all you love to economic slavery by corporate greed and communist economics! The answer is much more powerful than anything you've seen before. It is called the Great Majority Power Move! It is a simple move which enough of 300 million souls can repeat to gain overwhelming power over less than 600 souls in Washington. See it at: www.USAFreedom.us.

After four years in Iraq, America has nothing of value to show for it. The greatest war to win is the war of ideas. This one wins hearts and minds. This war could have saved much in cash and American lives. This war could have been won if our leaders only knew what to say. They are not any where near knowing what to say – OBVIOUSLY! If our president can't say enough good in America to win hearts, how can we expect him to say enough good in Iraq? Without winning hearts and minds in Iraq, military-might won't win either! In my opinion, if our leaders can't show enough responsibility to win the most basic part of this war, they don't deserve to be trusted to take care of the very costly military part either.

After four years, the government in Iraq is still very corrupt. The majority of Iraqis don't want our U.S. presence there. We've given four years of huge spending and American lives and we are nowhere near changing the will of the people in Iraq to end the chaos. As important as it is to secure safety in that region, it also doesn't make sense to repeat failure! It also doesn't make sense to economically rebuild another country while the same needs to be done right at home first!

P.S. - America will need to learn FAST the following lessons or face America's worst nightmare:

How to prosper a nation opposite to every failure and expense!

How to use other than terrorist fuel!

How to keep eating by growing food!

How to work children physically so they can grow smart mentally!

How to replace bad government with good government!

How to expose the corrupt and vote in the good!

How to return to traditional values rather than live in poverty to the lead of communist economics and exploitation by the few!

How to replace a bad election system by re-installing a representative form of government!

All of these MUST happen FAST if you don't want to be living America's worst nightmare!

Answers to all of the above are found at: www.USAFREEDOM.us.

What To Do With 14 Million Illegals

Let them find their way home the same way they came! This will happen when the legal place to work is back home! U.S. citizens wanting to keep illegal family members here can do so out of their own pocket. Those who go back to Mexico can also visit U.S. family members with legal passports. This way, they can visit family just like Americans do when traveling to visit family living elsewhere.

There is no reason why 14 to 20 million illegals should be allowed to receive financial support from the U.S. social security system and health care system that U.S. tax payers pay for from funds they will need! Politicians are stealing other people's money to get more votes by soft selling illegal immigration. That vote only supports more slavery.

Money speaks! Illegal immigration is mostly about exploitation of workers through slave labor wages. Ending exploitation is how to benefit workers of both countries. End exploitation and slave labor wages by ending illegal immigration. Unethical profit from slave labor is driving illegal immigration. Illegal immigration and slavery must go!

How To Restore The Greatest Nation – The Models

Why Remake America's National Economy

Economic policy is the means to all other policy, marriage, family, children, education, livelihood, health care, military, political, spiritual and more. Fix economic policy and others can be fixed. Let it go to the low price of China and all else will look like China!

Managing a national economy is manageable. Managing a global economy to the low price of China is not. The global economy will ruin you! All who know anything about direction will know that is true!

It makes no sense to compete with the likes of communist China and other third world thinking when all that remains is more third world competition, poverty, economic slavery, and other forms of slavery. Great subjects like marriage, family, children, child education, and livelihood are all served when our national economy is managed right.

With current policy, there's no way up but down. Our manufacturing, jobs, and technology are going overseas and leaving nothing to replace it. We have nothing to lose and everything to gain by changing direction. Dramatic change is needed. Majority response will do it!

Strengthening our economic borders is #1. Can it be done? It can if we try. I know we can't if we don't! There are excellent options!

Currently, those managing our economy are managing it like a pack of wolves rather than managers. They are failing by every standard!

We need balance between employer and worker, business and consumer, manufacturer and service, export and import. Apparently balance is not taught at Yale. I think we should also teach love for our neighbor.

When America competes with low wage countries like China and their great big global super store, there's no way up but down!

I support managing a national economy so there is balance and equality between company and worker, business and consumer, humanity and economics, manufacturing and service, exports and imports, rather than exploitation and other forms of economic slavery.

I support legislation and tax practices for doing it. It can be done with the same accuracy as a surgeon's knife. Implement tax practices favoring those who work versus favoring the very rich. Legislation should protect our jobs and economic borders. Both require a show of will! 300 million can change the corrupt system FAST!

Will America Or China Lead?

Also, will freedom lead or will communist China lead with human economic slavery and poverty?

Will China's leaders do a better job managing communist economics or will America's leaders do a better job managing sound business practice built on the golden rule - treating others how they'd like to be treated?

Will America's majority stand up for freedom and good for all and insist on the management of good over evil or will they ignore this message and be consumed with trivia and communist rule?

Will the majority be swayed by the glitter, glamour, and same old promises from the "do nothing" stars of failure from two failed political parties or will the majority take it upon themselves to talk with others about this cause and awaken the giant! All doing their part to tell family, friend, and neighbor, is the answer for dramatic change and total improvement. Talk the USAFreedom.us website, and my book, "Returning to America" which is power over failure? Either America or China will lead and affect the whole world! It is up to all of us to lead!

Taming The Corporate Beast

Tame corporate greed that is toxic to humanity, toxic to business, and toxic to everything about freedom! Greed happens when over-rich pay plans fail to have parody with other essential parts of a local and national economy. The parts must fit together in order to have a successful economy. There can't be some parts ravaging other parts through predatory practice.

America's great beginning was built on family business, family practice, family values, and family living. Business also reflected those values in the way all had common bond and all were treated like family. It was the golden rule in America. America can have this plan again! It comes from putting freedom first before economic slavery! All helping others can get it done!

Today, unreal expectations and over-rich pay plans are spelling trouble for America's future. I support balance, parody, equality, and guidance to bring us back to a working economy and people working again.

I support economic policy with direction, equality, and fairness. I also support policy which supports working people versus giving all of the benefit to those at the top. It happens with a sound national economy managed to do so. See my page on the model for remaking the economy.

America needs leaders who understand there is a problem with greed. These leaders also need courage to fix it!

I support business practices which are sustainable for the long run and good for people and good for business. This kind of business economics offers a sustainable and bright future. The other way is trash and burn. With the current trash and burn, everyone loses.

I support tax practices favoring working people over the very rich. I support measures which remove incentive from greed. This includes implementing federal pricing regulations to bring the economy back into workable balance with value exchanged for value.

I also support measures to prioritize national trade policies versus global trade with partners like China and the communist version of competition, poverty, and economic slavery.

I OPPOSE sending national business, national manufacturing, and national jobs over seas.

I support balance and equality in business both from employers and employees so America can move ahead in freedom versus slavery. It will happen with less greed and more sustainable pricing and pay practices. America can live better with less greed and more teamwork and concern for one another.

Greed is like a spoiled little child. It needs to be brought into check - wherever it exists!

I support taming the corporate beast.

For taming the corporate beast, see more at: www.USAFreedom.us

Saving Social Security

A top financial advisor would show the following to his clients regarding the financial choices they would make. This financial view puts all options on the table in order to make wise choices to SAVE SOCIAL SECURITY.

There are three places to invest money.

1. Stocks – ownership in companies for profit

2. Bonds – ownership in debt (promises to pay)

3. Cash – guaranteed money

Money in the social security trust fund now is guaranteed money.

Bonds are debt investments based on promises to pay back borrowed money.

Stocks are ownership in companies made for profit.

All throughout history, cash has been the worst investment of all. Even though it is guaranteed, inflation does more to destroy the value of money and its purchasing power more than any other factor.

Those promoting the safety of guaranteed money in social security system are promoting a bankrupt system certain to fail the future needs of today's children. This is due to the worst risk of all, inflation and failure to grow money!

Stocks are ownership in companies. The President wants to make it available to invest future earnings into stocks. This is no new idea to ANY sound investment program. Those opposed to this idea are giving you false advice on the most fundamental issue of sound investing.

The best part of investing is compounding interest. Here earnings earn earnings on earnings. This is how money earns much more money.

Here is one solid fact about investing. Stock investments are MUCH MORE likely to profit than guaranteed cash in the bank. If companies in general did not make more money than guaranteed cash in the bank, our financial system would collapse. Then, whatever we did wouldn't matter anyway!

By ALL statistics, the youth of today need the compounding earnings of stock investments like never before! This is why guaranteed money in the social security trust fund as is now, is the worst place for today's youth!

P.S. – Shouldn't professional advice rather than politicians guide choices regarding the future of social security?

I support privatizing social security for today's younger retirement "investors" so they enjoy the best compounding earnings history from ownership in stocks versus the other - guaranteed cash with the worst earnings record! This follows very prudent investment advice. Invest for compounding interest which stocks earn best!

If funds from social security were invested in stocks, there would also be more investment capital available for American companies. This would generate more jobs and prosperity in America!

For our children's sake, how about bringing this message to voters with clarity and purpose so social security for children is saved and not swept under the political carpet!

I also support this policy. "Say something constructive or nothing at all." Those who oppose this constructive solution should either offer at least the equivalent or say nothing at all!

Beat Big-money Politics

A single, well-placed stone conquered Goliath. The same is ours to repeat if we so choose for greatest success including winning back our country from a large corrupt giant.

America's Goliath is the political system bought and paid for by big money. This Goliath tells good-hearted American's "You can't have the kind of leadership you want in Washington! You can only choose from inside of the box of common failure with choices you don't want from the political system you don't want!" The truth is, Goliath can't give you what you want because Goliath is corrupt and filled with big money special interests, not yours! This message reveals what no other has, the answer on the other side of big money.

Some tell me, "You don't have a chance against this big corrupt giant!" They are looking at the giant. I am looking at the stone. The stone is the message of empowerment which speaks to the majority with no special interest. The message is far more compelling than both democrat and republican combined. The message about the stone comes from the mastermind of all success and the genius of all politics and every other subject. He is our Creator, the author all success, and also our mentor. His teachings are most effective yesterday, today, and forever for how to negotiate with the devil and win, how to shut the mouth of lions and accusers, how to speak a message which changes the world, and how to live the ultimate dreams by going opposite to every failure! The stone is His message which exposes the greatest evil and empowers with the greatest good. I'm repeating that message. This is my stone!

My message at www.LifeStylersUSA.com and www.USAFreedom.us speaks it like no politician has. The content is real with real answers for solving the largest political topics. When this message is heard through out major media, I think it will win hearts and minds of democrats, republicans, and all of us combined. A nation divided against it self cannot stand. Without the message about the stone, neither democrat nor republican can win each other, neither can they triumph over evil. Our future requires that we join forces in order to stand against the greatest evil lurking at our door. That evil is coming from a new and deadly economic system of global corporate greed, communist economics, and the most impoverished thinking from around the globe. It is time to redo our system beyond a surface fix like those in Washington offer. I want to ask democrats, republicans, and all of us combined to drop everything trivial and do our top task – protect our borders and save our children and our future from the worst of giants. Without a total fix, a surface fix is dead in the water even before it arrives! So what do we do to change the system and elect right leaders?

The greatest good is found on the other side of failure. The answer is a single well-placed stone representing great genius working in America's majority. From inside of the box, it would appear that the only option is to vote for more failure! Those inside of the box say it takes $10,000,000.00 dollars to run for president. You can't afford that any more than you can afford corrupt politicians! It is time to redo the election system and elect leaders who represent the majority. Rather than buy something we can't afford, I suggest we do what is affordable to win back freedom and our future for the majority. The answer is as simple as the stone. It works opposite to big money. It happens with a small $20.00 investment rather than $10,000,000.00. For that, you get the best-looking shirt in America with the website address on it for conquering giants. The website (www.USAFreedom.us) contains the greatest intelligence in presidential domain and the capacity to email others free this potent message for achieving real reform. Also, I will be working with all major media to promote the message. Also included are fifteen hard-hitting editorials which can be sent to local and national newspapers for printing. All of the above and this book come at a great low price opposite to way you don't like. All of it is FREE except for the book and the shirt but since you have to wear a shirt anyway it might as well be "Freedom". To get yours, order on-line at: www.USAFreedom.us. Your choice! Let the power of Goliath grow through silence or promote the message which conquers him!

National Economic Management vs. Global Economic Mismanagement

National economics is manageable! Global economics is not. Global competition to the lead of communist China and other third world thinking is chaotic at best and poverty at its worst! If you don't like communist China economics and China's other policies in your neighborhood and family, this message has the solution for change!

This message is reason to adopt a real economic policy for America. Currently, there is no management to manage. Currently, our policy is being managed by greed and the low price of communist economics!

Economic solution comes from managing our own economy. Managing our own economy is much more manageable than following every low price around the world. This is better than directing America's whole economic policy toward the low price of the child labor state of China and the rest of their policy.

While America's economic policy is serving communist China economics, America is losing in family, family values, child education, jobs with decent pay, and every subject most important to humanity.

Simple things like family, family values, marriage, and children are not above a president. They are the essence of him in how he shapes his country!

Currently, America's manufacturing and jobs are being gutted on the watch of America's elected officials. Obviously, these guys have never managed a business and they can't manage an economy either! I support bringing humanity back to America with marriage, family, children, livelihood, and economy at the center for a better economy!

I support a national economy which serves freedom over the global economy so we don't continue competing with poverty.

I support the kind of president who will put the needs of his nation before global competition with slavery!

I support a nation which models freedom and not slavery to the world by showing the world how one nation takes care of its own through sound national economic management.

Home Of The Brave, Land Of The Free

Home of the brave comes from those who have guts to get something done! Land of the free comes from those who are brave because they won't tolerate economic slavery and are willing to do what it takes to fix it!

With current policy, America is facing the worst economic nightmare progressing quickly toward us. It is based on communist China economics. This is a loose term describing the few at the top who exploit their own for money and other reasons!

The key to keeping economic freedom in America is to seek deep reform. Build the future on ageless, proven principles and values which are proven to work best for fair business, sound economics, and sound business practice.

Together, we can rebuild our economy based on the most traditional business practices most beneficial to all. This is an economy worth pursuing. It is all about serving those within our own borders! We did it once and we can do it again. We can also show others countries around the world how to do it and remain free!

It happens with national economics rather than global China economics. National economics is manageable. Global economics with the poor standards of China is not. There is nothing wrong with having global partners who show respect for human values and do not tolerate abuse of workers but national economy comes first!

I support gathering in the greatest power of teamwork with America's most brilliant minds and brilliant hearts to renew the nation of our dreams!

I support rebuilding our economic infrastructure to serve America and freedom. It includes freedom from the destructive nature of greed in business and government! The other way is not working!

When human values and humanity are gone, there is nothing left - not even human values for the greedy!

The only way America can have freedom again is to have a home of the brave! Please help rebuild America's business and economy along freedom lines!

I support a free society built on the golden rule in business. This includes fair taxing and fair business practice. This practice benefits fairly all those who work in a free national economy. I also support having enough leadership in government to encourage and oversee fairness!

All of the above are opposite to what we are getting! This is your home! Are you brave?

Real Education Policy For Children

America's children are losing the most vital lessons in education by the same means America is losing economically by competing with the child labor state of China. Children are losing the true foundation to education. The true foundation comes from marriage, family, livelihood, and sound economic policy. These touch every part of children's lives.

How about having a real education policy and be world leaders in human values at the same time! Give children a nation with a balanced, managed, national economy where there is not the low price of China in their lives. Teach them how to enjoy life so they develop passion for all that life offers. Passion for things they enjoy will improve their learning.

Hectic hurried schedules of academia are good for nothing when children miss the most real themes of living.

Give children love and acceptance and not all of the competition from over-seas which is adding stress to family life and turning children into used academia.

Build passion for life and interest in relationships.

Education without love, acceptance, and enjoyment of life is good for nothing.

Remember when children had more time for fun, self-awareness, self-identity, and family relationships? Today's children are too busy for that with homework assignments and busy schedules. Is this sounding a little bit communist?

They are also missing that very important part of life which makes them whole. Show them that everything isn't about school and sports and a brand of performance constantly measuring their worth. They are already priceless! Love them for being children and have simple fun with them in the simple beauties of life to broaden their perspective.

Their greatest lesson is your time to tell them they are worth it. Also, teach them the value of having a love mission worth giving their all for. It can start with parents by loving God, family, neighbor, and country.

For real education for children, I support bringing America's business leaders back home to the country of human values where life can be good for all children and everyone. This is a plan where children can prosper in a better way than China can give. I support fiscal policy which discourages them from leaving. I support appealing to their humanity and showing them that no one has a future where human values and the land of the free are gone! Right leadership will say the right words and inspire significant change!

Let's tell our business leaders to protect our children from global competition built by China's business policy where they have no time for life's finer lessons! This means, America must stop competing with third world thinking to keep up with poverty. This means, educating children first in how to take care of children so they can take care of responsibilities when they grow up.

For the education of children, I support protecting our economic borders. These are also our character borders. The communist way where human values crumble is no way to build anything!

George Bush's plan to improve math and science in school won't happen until love in the family is renewed all over America and we know how to count fairness for our fellow man in livelihood. This is the foundation for real education for children!

Why USAFreedom.us Is The Answer

A football team wins if the receiver is at the right place on the field at the right time to catch the winning pass?

This answer is also true for us as Americans to win back the nation of our dreams. Can America win if Americans don't have the right mind-set to win and catch the ball?

Our best way to win is to play on a team and do everything required of winning? Winning is also the best course for having most fun!

The ball has been thrown. We are in the biggest game of our lives! It is about saving the nation of our dreams from economic poverty to the lead of big-money exploitation, communist economics, and other forms of global poverty! America is our world, the world which makes up every part of our lives and surrounds all of us!

We can win with the greatest ease! Play together as a team and play with passion like others have for sports! 300 million with minimal effort will overpower five hundred and thirty six in Washington.

Winning has always happened when individuals decided to rally around most compelling ideas and values. Individuals and small groups have always played a vital role in changing the course of history. It is our time to shine. You can be one who makes a difference!

The majority can promote freedom's cause with ease with a message beyond politics and beyond the media! Email the message of USA Freedom to others. What will happen if every person does and each reaches ten others? Also, wear a Fashion of Freedom shirt so hundreds and thousands can view it. Also, buy more copies of this book and give them to others to spread the message. This is the way to spread answers and inspire change! This is a way to support economic freedom and prosperity for America over economic poverty and other forms of slavery! This is why USA Freedom is the answer!

U.S.A. Freedom vs. U.N. Slavery

Most of the world is blind to the facts about the U.N. It would be a world disaster to trust the U.N. with power to run world matters like so many trust the U.N. Preventing the world's largest political disaster coming from the world's largest ignorance is why this message is needed.

Freedom comes from heeding the U.S. Constitution and truth. Truth shows how to win. Slavery comes from U.N. delegates who don't have values of truth and don't have knowledge of truth to protect freedom!

This message shows why it is impossible for the U.N. to work as a model government. The same also reveals why the U.N. is fine for administering world food programs but a dangerous deception to trust to manage world issues. Also, see in this message a better way to trust.

You've heard it called the new world order. Ignorance is the only reason for trusting the U.N. with such power. See why this organization is the largest idea ever devised for failure and slavery. Also see why the U.N. is completely incapable of continuing freedom like you currently enjoy and perhaps take for granted.

Here is why! Every successful organization needs members who share common ways and common values. The U.N. has neither. America, the world, and freedom needed to see that. Can you imagine one organization formed from the greatest array of cultures and self-interests?

Is there any surprise that U.N. delegates cannot work together to gain agreement on important matters like protecting freedom?

Second, giving trust to U.N. leaders the way they desire gives the power away and makes the give-away practically impossible to reverse. Note that the power hungry model of the U.N. is to RULE THE MATTERS OF THE WORLD!

Should people of freedom foolishly give the U.N. such trust like many are mentally positioned to do, this would be the turning point for freedom, a point of no return - never again to return to BALANCE OF POWER given in the U.S. Constitution! Even now, some U.S. Senators blindly give more trust to the U.N. government than they do to their own. Watch out for their justification. It is called "international law".

Since when did the U.N. become the god of justice? Those who serve this god will find it more appropriately called the god of failure and slavery!

Keep in mind the U.S. Constitution is filled with balance of power. If this balance is disturbed, you start losing balance of power and freedom. Choose America's constitution or lose it forever to all kinds of strange third world thinkers who don't know what freedom is about.

Let the world rise to U.S. Constitutional standards rather than lowering U.S. standards to theirs!

Third, this organization is not trust-worthy. Most people wouldn't marry a stranger or trust a stranger to baby-sit their children. How could trust in U.N. delegates to run your world be any different?

Fourth, as much as you would like to believe in a perfect world, world peace, and the U.N. to give it to you, don't be fooled. These perfectly fallible figures of men in the U.N. have a perfect record of failure for doing this. Furthermore, they are blind! Why? Because they are void of truthful standards. Without truth, they are blind and cannot see.

Excuse me for my political incorrectness here but how would you like your life run by leaders of China, Iran, Africa, and others, who sit in plush ivory towers while their people starve to death in streets and in political prisons?

Since when do you want to partner with complete heathen thinkers like this who think nothing of implementing policies which completely abuse human rights and personal freedom? What part of their lies do you want for your life? If America, the world, and freedom don't grasp this message, all may find themselves living under U.N. control with no way out.

Government Of The People - Part Two

I believe most Americans want personal empowerment more than government politics. The most rewarding course in personal empowerment happens by reclaiming government of the people, by the people, and for the people. Do this and the lessons you gain will transform you in every most empowering way!

Currently, many regard our politicians and lobbyist as the majority! On the contrary, our population of 300 million is the majority. The ratio is 300 million to less than 600 or 500,000 to one. What intelligence would not appreciate this opportunity?

I support waking the giant! The giant is the people parts when the people assemble in strength as one! Rise up in personal leadership and empowerment to remake the nation of our dreams – a nation with sound economic policy and much more. Awaken the majority and everything can be fixed. Also show your children what parenting is all about by showing them your might and stand for freedom. This is government of the people, by the people, and for the people.

By standing together as one, we have every opportunity to improve our nation for all of freedom's children. The other choice is to let China rule the world with low price, their competition, and economic slavery! Government of the people, by the people, and for the people is our answer including most amazing lessons of personal empowerment. This lesson in practice will serve our every desire!

The best happens by solving the largest problems.

By taking interest in solving very large matters, we can think outside of the box to find really great answers.

Some of the answers include love for family, friend, and neighbor, speaking with others about making positive change, building teamwork, and having a love mission the size of our nation. These are all material for outstanding personal empowerment!

Contrary to most common thoughts of unbelief and defeat, the greatest battles before us can be won. They can be won by gathering together in the power of one and by exchanging great ideas among us. What could be greater for every future? This is government of the people, by the people, and for the people!

Our government is what it is because of us. Our duty is to make government what we want. I support telling our elected officials we want the country of our dreams back rather than economic slavery to the low price of China. This happens by electing leaders who will manage our national economy just like every smart businessperson manages business. The other choice is to lie down in hopeless failure and let the low price of China rule the world with the Chinese version of economic slavery.

Government Of The People - Part Three

America's freedom is under attack by career bureaucrats in government. They are using and abusing the power of government for personal self-gain.

I support the will of the people to remake government of the people, by the people, and for the people for the good of all. Eliminate from office those in government who promote the practice of slavery. We have a political process in our constitution to do just that.

Our government is what it is because of us and it is our duty to make it what we want! Our choice is to stand up for freedom or lie down and let a small minority roll over us with financial and political greed.

By sheer numbers, the majority can win over the small minority by simply engaging government of the people, by the people, and for the people. Let's show our children how fun it is to gather with other special people who love freedom and success just like we do! Isn't this the right crowd for you to be running with?

Government should never be about democrat or republican. It should always be about the will of the people and a grass roots campaign of the people. In the next election, each of us will either vote for apathy or energy. I much prefer energy because America can have a bright future with a great show of energy! If we don't take this opportunity to change direction, we will support slavery by accepting the current direction.

Change can start immediately by talking about keeping freedom over slavery. Also, tell others about this website. Tell ten others to tell ten others and ask each of them to tell ten others. This is grass roots at its finest! What could be more vital for keeping freedom?

I also support changing the system of corruption in government in simple, doable ways. The "Walk for America" and the "The 2007 Petition for America" are two places to start.

Let's talk among 300 million about personal empowerment like we haven't heard from Washington!

Government Of The People - Part Four

Economic policy is the financial means to every other policy.

Our U.S. workers cannot complete with the low price of human slavery in China without having plenty of human slavery of our own.

One doctor told me he likes our economy just the way it is and he opposes federal regulation of our economy. He said he hates the thought of government regulation on pricing. He believes federal regulation is a form of dictatorship. Of course he would!

Most other Americans have to negotiate the price of their goods and services! Doctors simply dictate their charges. I think doctors should do well but not so well that they break the economic souls of their patients. If doctors continue abusing middle class people who work, they won't have a country! I would like to see doctors become rich by treating their neighbors as they would like to be treated. America can no longer afford doctor dictators.

Some doctors are earning more in one week than their patients earn all year!

This is happening while our government leaders are selling American jobs over seas. Some doctors are charging $500.00 to $1000.00 or more per hour. Credit card companies are charging annual interest rates of up to 30% or more. And now if you get sick, you could lose your life if you can't pay the good doctor in up-front cash!

Our constitution calls for life in America without fear. Our government leaders have been doing nothing to improve health care. They have also done nothing to stop financial rape of America's patients. Our government leaders are being careless and irresponsible with America's constitutional right to live without fear.

I support having a nationally balanced economy. Government regulation is now giving all of the financial benefit to big money lobbyist in health care in ways which break the middle-class soul. This is poor regulation!

I support new direction in government run by those who understand small business. In my opinion, small business experience is needed most for America far more than large corporate monopolies. Our government leaders today are destroying small business now just like they have destroyed small family farms.

Obviously, America doesn't' need more of the same from big-money monopolies managing our country. We already have that.

Right federal regulation is the answer. Regulation by itself is neither bad nor good. It all depends on how it is used and how it functions as either bad or good. The current system, with all of the above, is bad!

P.P.S. - I support gaining one large prize that is more important than individual profession or income. That prize is gaining control of our government and nation so all don't find themselves living under corporate extortion or communist rule. Only government regulation and skilled economic management can stop that. Majority power can do it and improve direction. A minority of the self-serving may not agree.

Saving Health Care

Two solutions to saving health care costs are shown here! One solution is more political while the other is more practical.

The political solution replaces third party billing with the original honest plan - single payer direct billing. This option simply takes political will in Washington to do by favoring patients rather than the lobby groups, insurance companies, pharmaceutical companies, and health care providers.

The single payer system was common practice before third party billing. With single-payer direct billing, the patient is the single payer. The bill comes directly from the health care provider to the patient. This is a simple formula. Direct billing encourages responsible billing based on real life economics and real-life relationship between the health care provider and the patient. Third party billing is the opposite. It accommodates irresponsible billing and extortion because neither health care provider nor insurance companies feels personal responsibility to charge reasonable prices because billing is so impersonal. As a result, both are party to exorbitant billing, exorbitant profits, and extortion at the expense of the public. Third party billing is a convenient way for insurance companies and health care providers to be less accountable to serve the economic needs of patients. As a result, health care charges are fixing the body and breaking the soul! Too many doctors are earning more in one week than their patients earn all year. This is the case with third party billing. This is one more example of exploitation of the majority by the few and Washington politicians know it.

The second way to save health care cost is very practical.

This plan offers potential cost savings far greater than any recent president has offered. You will see here how pennies can save dollars. This is very good news for America's economy in every way!

The answer? Empower each and every American, a whole country, to make right choices where it counts most in saving health care! It has to do with what goes into the body daily which can either be very healthy or very unhealthy. Healthy daily choices can positively impact our whole economy in every way! The benefits are huge and most gratifying to every person with a long list of lifestyle benefits! Here is how!

Before now, the health care fix has been nothing more than political rhetoric in Washington. Talk alone doesn't help anyone. The political solution in Washington leaves the every day person powerless with no answer and no direction. I support making health care a personal issue where much can be done to solve the real issues of protecting health. These are real solutions provided at home at the roots before health care becomes expensive.

Without personal responsibility, education, and new direction, our nation faces crippling health care costs within just one short decade.

Consider all of the junk food that is sabotaging America's future! I support an education policy filled with missing answers and missing parts of motivation for saving health and health care costs nationally.

This plan has three steps, accountability, responsibility, and mostly empowerment!

I support accountability, responsibility, and mostly EMPOWERMENT for each person to accept responsibility for their own health. No one wants to absorb health care costs for others who continually violate their own health and health care savings? No one can afford that! Neither can government!

I support personal accountability and responsibility for personal health. I also believe in providing choices to eliminate personal senseless expense. EMPOWERMENT is the answer!

I support federal spending for public education so all are empowered with prevention and healthy living. Pennies invested here can save dollars. I also support hiring top education and motivation experts to bring home the message about saving health care cost through healthy living.

Ignorance is presently the king dominating health care expense. It is a big problem being glazed over by those in Washington.

I support federal regulations to put limits on charges for health care.

I support price caps on medical damages to eliminate price gouging by lawyers. America can no longer afford costly lawsuits.

I support adding more health care professionals to eliminate shortages, exorbitant demand, and exorbitant charges for service.

I support cost saving measures within the means of government (some are not being utilized which already exist) to provide stop-loss health care the private sector is not able to fill.

I support improving our agricultural industry and stimulating our economy at the same time to serve the needs of America locally and nationally where the healthiest choices are found on freedom soil.

I support electing leaders in America who can generate more passion for health and more savings in health care! I support starting at home where America draws its strength! This is what I support for top health care savings!

Liberty And Justice For All

Freedom comes with liberty and justice for all. Start abusing liberty and justice, and slavery starts.

America needs to revitalize justice and make people pay in the ways they don't want for crimes against liberty and justice.

Execute those who commit intolerant crimes and be much less tolerant. America can no longer afford our expensive judicial system.

Physical laws and financial laws need to serve liberty and justice for all. We can't be spiritual and have freedom when we abuse the physical laws of liberty and justice for all.

It doesn't make sense to take food and health care from those who work and support families while giving those benefits to the worst of criminals instead. That's slavery!

I support holding politicians and lawyers personally responsible. Demand that they make changes to serve America rather than slavery!

I support adding new laws with new reach to correct the culture of lying, cheating, and stealing in business. I support power for law enforcement to make it illegal and highly unpleasant to sabotage the culture of honest business and economy.

I support turning bulging prison populations into profitable people. It happens by turning our prison systems into productive business centers for profit. This policy can rehabilitate those who can be by giving them real skills needed to provide. It can also be good for the business of corrections. Business partners on the outside can also profit from this venture.

I support making a real difference for honest people

I support liberty and justice for all!

Here are steps to liberty and justice for all: Email freedom messages to family, friend, neighbor, and those with many contacts. This is happening all around America! Buy the "Freedom" shirt to promote the message. Tell others about this book and share it with friends, neighbors, and key public figures. Put freedom is in the hands of those who want it. Take measures to protect freedom like your future depends on it! It really does! I know freedom is no longer in the hands of republicans or democrats!

Protecting Our Hunting Heritage

America's hunting heritage includes a long history of relationship with self, family, friend, and God in nature. This kind of foundation you will see is the great foundation to America and to our future. Nothing gets better than the real life themes of God and His nature. Hunting is one real way to celebrate this nature with friend, family, and neighbor. Protecting our hunting heritage is also about our choice to raise children on hunting and fishing to find real-life lessons equal to the game. The other choice is to continue the course of TV screens and computer monitors where nothing is real.

In nature, all senses are tuned to the game! With the other, five senses learning is not needed and neither is the game. Hunting not only quickens brain cells with a full course in five senses learning, but it also teaches basic child-like talents like enthusiasm, optimism, and keen site for the game!

At this important time when America's students are falling behind in academics, America is also losing economically at the risk of collapse. With all of the failure from the above conditions, there is also a thriving TV and computer culture. Ever consider the parallels? On the other hand, the common link in Nobel Prize Winners is their common child-hood link to nature and animals.

In the very beginning, God gave man dominion over the earth to manage it. Management over nature is a powerful responsibility and a powerful course of learning. What could be greater for America and children than to keep the heritage of hunting alive and well with lessons equal to the maker?

It happens in relationships while hunting in nature. It also happens with balance between predators and prey so predators don't kill everything including our heritage!

Healing The Nation: The Plan Is Ready

This plan is an invitation to individuals and organizations nationwide to join together as one in strength and unity for freedom's cause.

Have you ever seen a team go to the top without standing together? Our victory is no different! We must stand together if we want to win the challenges facing us. This plan makes it simple!

The other option is to ignore this message and see the continued downfall of our life and nation in more hurtful, divisive, destructive ways hurting everyone and costing everyone in very expensive ways.

Four Steps To Healing A Nation

Preface: In just 70 years, from 1900 to 1970, communism gained control of two-thirds of the world population by the strength of single-minded focus. Now, America has more compelling reason for unity. The reason is preserving freedom and saving our nation from the same militant power. Single-minded focus is the key.

1. Website - One place, one site for America to place her eyes for single-minded focus. www.USAFreedom.us is the place on the web about freedom and sowing America together on issues eroding freedom. By linking the information and experience of knowledgeable concerns nationally, www.USAFreedom.us provides rare perspective

and reason for America to stand up with diligence for freedom. The purpose for this website is to harness the strength of the nation to keep freedom a priority. Single-minded focus of individuals and organizations is the key to power and influence. As the efforts of many combine, America can once again have the strength, confidence, and conviction to keep constitutional freedom.

2. Message shirts which advertise this website are available to individuals and organizations for local and national distribution. These shirts serve three functions: **One:** Offer an elite look that is truly attractive as a fashion of freedom. **Two:** Communicate a message for raising public awareness to the issues. **Three:** Below each message, promote the web address and site for super powerful single-minded focus on issues important for continuing freedom. One shirt in a crowd can deliver a message to hundreds and thousands of viewers.

3. Email will effectively advertise www.USAFreedom.us through thought provoking, appealing, non-partisan messages. At the end of each message, the website address follows with access to powerful website information. This place on the web will efficiently and effectively educate great numbers of Americans nationwide to issues of freedom. Whole organizations, with memberships of two to twenty million, will have easy access to reach their members from the top down with a send key. Organization directors can email to their members. They in turn can email to family and friends, and family and friends can e-mail to other family and friends until all have heard.
www.USAFreedom.us is a voice for America beyond politics or the evening news. There is time before the next election to empower America with an appealing message. With this, America can have a message of her own reflecting her priceless worth.

4. The slogan for America's freedom is www.USAFreedom.us. The power of this slogan is in the size - so small it can fit anywhere and be seen everywhere to bring the eyes of America together. The slogan provides single-minded focus for the purpose of unifying and healing the nation. The slogan website communicates most effectively by the

power of truth and goodness among us. The message with the slogan will not build walls of defense or divide a nation. Instead, it will embrace all with truth. The slogan will be viewed again and again in public places. To all who see, it will serve as a reminder that America has a voice for freedom!

www.USAFreedom.us will be seen on shirts at public events. It will be seen on car windows and bumpers. It will be emailed among family and friends and much, much more. By God's grace and goodness, it will change hearts, souls, and minds and all will be better for it. - www.USAFreedom.us

P.S. - To benefit you, your family, friends, church, business, organization, and nation, please feel free to choose - buy a shirt, promote a shirt, e-mail a message, and pass along a website address.

Healing The Nation Starting With Truth

The Constitution of the United States has been the foundation to the greatest nation on earth. It has also been the foundation to the greatest freedom. The greatest threat to this freedom is ignorance of truth because the U.S. Constitution comes from principles of truth in the Bible. Ignorance of truth is common as evidenced by all of life's failure. This same ignorance can cause free people to foolishly squander freedom and trade it for trust in the governments of men.

The Bible warns against trusting in men (and their institutions). - Instead, trust in God and the goodness He has placed within us to know truth and overcome evil with good.

* Rather than dwelling on negatives and complaining, we can take positive action and overcome evil with good.
* Rather than waiting for politicians and others to make us happy, we can take initiative to overcome evil with good and change situations through the power of good.

* Rather than waiting to be served by government, we can look to serve and profit from serving.
* Rather than blaming others for wrong, we can look within to find the goodness of God that enables us to overcome injustice.
* Rather than competing with others as enemies, we can embrace them in friendship, and by the power of goodness, win those who will stand with us.
* Rather than studying the evils of men and their shortcomings, we can study the perfection of God in the ways that individuals and nations become   strong.
* Rather than finding pleasure in greed, we can enjoy great riches through the kingdom of God that is within us.

Truth was, is, and always will be the answer to freedom. Governments will never be the answer to freedom. This is truth's purpose. Nothing can be more profound or appealing than truth itself. Trust inspired by truth is the way to start at the top and be free!

Why Vote For Leaders Who Know The Difference Between Good And Evil

Leaders throughout history have had the largest part in shaping the future for all people. Every thing rolls down hill. It starts with leaders! Choose leaders correctly or pay the highest price for leaders who don't know right from wrong and good from evil.

This message contains the most important information you will read pertaining to the leadership selection you will make in voting and deciding your future.

When the righteous are in authority, the people rejoice; but when the wicked rule, the people mourn. - Proverbs 29:2

The most dramatic information regarding good and evil has to do with a spiritual message about the greatest good and the worst evil. Both are clearly taught through Biblical knowledge. This message reveals truth about the greatest reality of life, the one with real reality behind every other reality. It is about the author of reality - God Himself. It also includes His knowledge regarding the difference between good and evil and how to choose leaders correctly to make right decisions and keep freedom!

Until leaders know truth, they can't really understand the difference between good and evil and how to separate the difference. This also means their leadership is flawed because they are naïve to the influence of good and evil. When leaders know the truth of God about good and evil, they also know the power of good to overcome evil. Their leadership will also be marked by powerful influence because large numbers of people will find them worthy to follow.

Vote for leaders who know what truth is!

The Real Reason For Guns In America

The real reason for guns is not to be confused with or watered down by less significant issues. Guns are not just for hunting even though hunting has huge benefits to society. Neither are guns mostly about anti-gun laws which protect children from accidental shootings. Neither are they about preventing high school kids from going on shooting rampages, or as a safety measure by policemen to make their jobs safer. All of the above are social issues. These go back to living right as parents and citizens to impact society right. If we are not honest with those social issues, they will never be resolved!

The real reason for guns is stated in the U.S. Constitution for the protection of freedom. This is what the U.S. Constitution is for.

The U.S. Constitution was written by America's forefathers who came from tyranny in Europe. These forefathers knew the lessons of history.

These lessons were also re-enforced by every real-life lesson these forefathers experienced first hand. What they saw from motherland Europe was deliberate political moves by individuals in the power of government and elsewhere to abuse the power of government to control others with evil, tyrannical ways.

Have we become so civilized that tyranny in government is no longer a concern? Only in a world of anti-reality by people who either don't care or don't understand the difference between good and evil! Guns will always have power to hold back the advances of evil because they hold the power of life and death.

There is no greater respect than that which holds the power of life and death! Guns keep respect. Guns also provide citizens with the power of good over potential domination by the worst of evil.

Simply put, guns are an ultimate tool of freedom. Could anyone deny such respect as well as the value of respect which guns deserve? Guns are America's way to manage evil silently, affordably, and harmlessly.

For those in government who desire to restrict the right to bear arms, they will find more value in the big picture instead! This is about the right of law-abiding citizens to protect from the worst potential evil so they are not deceived by smaller priorities.

America is the only great nation strong enough to protect freedom from the worst enemies of freedom. If America wants to keep freedom, America must protect freedom first on freedom soil. It starts on freedom soil as it has since the very beginning at the birth of freedom.

Times have not changed. The fact is, evil is still at work to hinder, damage, and destroy freedom in every way possible.

Freedom isn't free! The real reason for guns is to protect free people from harm. Freedom can continue as long as free people have guns.

P.S. - Politicians who don't believe in guns also don't believe in the goodness of people to have them. Don't give them your vote because they want to control you!

The Real Reason For Guns In America – Part Two

The real reason for guns in America is stated in the second Amendment of the U.S. Constitution. We often hear reference to the second amendment but here are the words and the meaning, lest we forget!

"A well regulated Militia, being necessary to the security of a Free State, the right of the people to keep and bear arms, shall not be infringed."

Also, the Declaration of Independence states … *"When in the Course of human Events, it becomes necessary for one People to dissolve the political Bands which have connected them with another, and to assume among the Powers of the Earth, the separate and equal Station to which the Laws of Nature and of Nature's God entitle them, a decent Respect to the Opinions of Mankind requires that they should declare the causes which impel them to the Separation."*

Clearly, guns are first to protect free people from the risk of oppressive government gone bad, either foreign or domestic. Any political spin meant to belittle this for lesser reason is deception.

Our Constitution requires us to do what is right even when the laws themselves fail to do what is right. Then, it is our duty to disobey for the sake of the good and change laws which need changing.

Your gun rights are being infringed as follows.

Your right to keep and bear arms without tyranny of fear of search and seizure of gun, car, house, or any other legal possession of yours by any government agency using the strategy of fear, tyranny, and/or oppression to govern you through victimizing law.

Your right to keep and bear arms, without infringement on those rights by state or federal law requiring you to register yourself, and your gun, and be required to pay oppressive renewal fees to in order to keep and bear your arms.

Your right to walk in nature with God, family, friend, and/or other to nurture every human relationship including fatherhood, motherhood, brotherhood, friendship, fellowship, and more by experience in nature. This would include walking with firearm of choice and living without fear while doing so while also protecting self, family, friends, and/or other from predator, or other hostile element. This is an unalienable right given by God without a small game license from the DNR. This is your right as an adult to keep and bear arms while enjoying every positive theme of God's green earth without being subject to passing a DNR hunter safety course.

Your nation's fate is mainly decided by your show of will! 300 million citizens have a golden opportunity now to remake government of the people by the simple deeds of the Great Majority Power Move. It happens by doing the same simple deeds together to end government corruption!

Freedom Is Free Only In An Anti-war, Anti-reality World!

The following describes a new anti-reality world of anti-war protestors, and measures America can take to safeguard freedom from present and future ignorance. Unless America returns to raising children on real life lessons and truth rather than televisions, computer monitors, and video games, this ignorance will continue to grow dangerous deception, wrong choices, and utter defeat opposite to freedom and everything good!

Remember when children commonly lived on family farms and family units were strong. Children had a real sense of reality because real life themes and real life lessons were all around them. These children were the product of the real life lessons they learned. They not only learned about people and relationships but, they also saw other real life themes including real animals, life and death, good and evil, and much more which was real. TV back then also had real human themes − forces of real good and real evil in people working against each other.

Today's children are not so blessed. Today's world has many more false realities shaping childhood learning. These falsehoods come from TV screens, computer monitors, video games, and other plastic world realities. In this world, children grow up to believe in cartoons heroes and animals that talk like humans.

The dangerous part about this new world ignorance is a dangerous new ignorance with very deadly consequences opposite to freedom, truth, and everything good. Why is it dangerous? Because this ignorance fails to reveal truth about right and wrong, good and evil, and other real matters.

Understand this new anti-reality world and you will understand the new anti-war generation. These people are a product of their learning and what they are learning has little to do with reality.

The following are realities they have not come to know.

The anti-reality generation has not learned lessons from history. If they knew history, they would know history's most potent lessons about America's forefathers who gave their lives so others could have freedom.

They also didn't learn lessons about good and evil. To miss calculate either is evil and dangerous for both the people of today and freedom for tomorrow.

Could any intelligent life form fail to recognize the power of evil and the influence of evil on life? Is the anti-war anti-reality generation so naïve as to think evil is now completely managed by U.N. officials? Or perhaps, do they want to give freedom away because they don't know how to manage it?

Have they completely missed histories lessons about the role of evil to possess, enslave, rape, torture, and kill? What kind of rose-colored glasses are they wearing?

Neither anti-war nor anti-reality have any power to stop evil. These perspectives only help the anti-reality people to blind their view before evil strikes. Do they think the world would be better off to ignore the brutality of men like Saddam Hussein and Ossama Bin Laden while their evil have children who grow and train more evil? Do anti-war people really think there is no reason to address evil?

Evil is an integral part of this life! It will always work as an enemy of freedom. This is why this life will always have war and need to fight wars for freedom.

Every great hero who has given life for freedom, and every war won to bring freedom to this remarkable place has been necessary for freedom. Now, let us not spoil freedom with ignorance and shortsighted thinking lest we destroy all we have gained. Without these past heroes and the wars that were fought, these anti-war protesters would not even be here to protest

How ironic that they would denounce the very reality which gives them freedom! We will keep freedom only if we keep protecting it!

Freedom is free only when you live in an anti-reality world!

The following is the secret to building a brighter future based on reality? It starts by replacing TV screens and computers monitors with real life themes of nature. Teach children how to enjoy nature sports with family. Enjoy hunting, fishing, camping, outdoor photography, and more in nature. Show children how to find pleasure in the real life themes of nature. Also teach them the difference between good and evil found in the Bible. This is life's most potent lesson. Without a knowledge of good and evil, individuals are blind, naïve, and ignorant.

For more about reshaping America in most rewarding ways, visit: www.LifeStylersUSA.com. All is worth nothing until it becomes lifestyle!

Freedom Without Discipline Is Bondage

How often have you observed those who believe in freedom yet, obviously fail in most practical ways? Why is this? Because freedom without discipline is bondage!

There is only one certain way to be free and enjoy freedom. The answer comes from personal discipline to do right according to truthful standards. Error doesn't work to keep freedom. Neither does failure. Free people cannot continue to remain free when they continue to repeat failure.

Jesus Christ said this in John 8:31-32.

If ye continue in my word, then, ye are my disciples indeed. And ye shall know the truth, and the truth shall make you free.

Have you seen how crazy people are without standards of truth? Have you seen how nutty they can really be? Truth is everyone's answer to freedom because it provides answers for winning rather than losing. There are certainly many people losing in many different ways aren't there?

Truth provides the intelligence to know how to win. It works by providing the right motives to begin everything right and finish every thing right to receive right results.

Lessons Of Life Animal Rights Groups Can't Teach

Family recreation, family values, family bonding, family education, and other great lessons, including relationship with God Himself, are all enriched through traditional outdoor activities. These are hunting, fishing, and more!

A new breed of ignorance never seen before in the history of mankind is attacking these same activities and the values which go with them. This is the new animal rights movement.

This movement has been growing in popularity in direct proportion to the new modern cartoon depictions of life. See below reason for ignorance and how to protect America from more damage.

See why the message animal rights groups are receiving through cartoons is dangerous and damaging to America and to all values which keep America free.

The lessons we learn are those which shape us most. Many of life's greatest lessons are learned from creation in nature and nature's real-life themes.

In the beginning God gave man dominion over the earth to manage it. Proper management skills include most valuable lessons of self-identify, self-esteem, self-awareness, awareness of others, leadership, initiative, and every positive human theme.

America's continued success depends upon these themes thriving in human intelligence. These themes are developed by personal involvement in outdoor activities. This includes hunting, farming, livestock management, and more which God gave to man to manage.
These lessons are under attack by a new breed of ignorance never seen before in the history of mankind. It is called the animal rights movement.

In my opinion, some work accomplished by animal rights groups is constructive. Safeguarding reasonable humane treatment of animals is one. Other work should be corrected for destroying human values, family values, and more by extremists still watching cartoons. Hunting and other natural harvest practices is a good place to start for showing respect for the roles of humans and human values.

Either overcome this ignorance with education or see a nation damaged and/or destroyed by ignorant legislation and laws which oppress the most fundamental lessons of life - lessons in wholeness. The best is real-life learning.

See how significant the lessons of nature are for America's children, families, and future.

How about embracing the exceptional learning opportunities in the real outdoors versus the common artificial culture of TV screens and computer monitors where nothing is real!

Images Made For Children

Winning for children is easy with positive mind images. For children, the images in the mind determine most their future. The following is about images of fantasy or images of truth children will come to know. Stories these images produce influence them, their future, and all they do. Today's parents have an opportunity to shape destiny for children based on truth. Here is how.

Give children images of real people doing real good. This is not about fantasy characters on TV which talk like humans and portray unreal images. The real heroes aren't elves, Easter bunnies, or artificial figures. Real-life heroes are real people our children can know and become. Here is one place to start. Read children Bible stories about real people doing real good. Teach them truth from the Bible, persistence, caring, and other good qualities. Also share real-life stories about every day heroes who overcome evil with good. Give our children real images they can trust and become. - A message for healing a nation.

The Influence Of TV On Children

One could hardly consider the welfare of children without also considering what they watch. They are watching about eleven hours of TV per week.

The following is a candid look at what is happening to a nation of children. Your question, "Do I want a nation of children (mine and others) to be a part of this crowd and how can I fix it?"

Eleven hours of TV represents eleven hours of prime time in a little life and prime time for bonding. With TV, children aren't bonding to parents and family or real-life themes. At best, they are bonding to cartoon heroes which talk like humans.

Cartoon heroes are a false reality they cannot trust. Since when are cartoons real? And since when do animals talk like humans? Cartoon makers are sparing nothing to load up artificial cartoon figures with human emotions and human appeal.

One thing leads to another and first thing you know, there is a whole new culture never seen before in the history of mankind; an anti-reality culture based on cartoon heroes and animals which think and talk like people.

Have we become more civilized or more deceived? Has the cartoon world brought people to a new way of thinking, a new reality which takes their emotions for a train ride and drops them off in world of disaster?

There is another option. Teach children how to know life for what it really is. This way they will have a belief system they can trust to be effective in real life situations!

There's Healing In The Soil

He that tilleth his land shall have plenty of bread: but he that followeth vain persons shall have poverty enough. – Proverbs 28:19

Our vain politicians through ignorant ways and total failure as leaders have destroyed the culture of the small family farm just like they are destroying now the culture of small business, family business, family practice in business, and family values in business. Just as it was destroyed, it can be built again with the right message and sound leadership. America has the land to do it, the resources to do it, and America needs the mind-set to do it – even if that means going bankrupt to the World Bank and the Chinese government to take back the land of the free! We can take our country back and not go into economic slavery to the worst exploiters, extortionists, traitors, treasonous minds, and ignorant minds in Washington.

Why risk food shortages, price gouging by corporate extortionists, and economic breakdowns in food supply like we will see in oil supply. The oil supply issue will affect every industry which oil supply affects which is every industry! Why not be a nation of self-sufficiency so we don't rely on other countries we don't trust? If we are self-sufficient, changes in relationship with other nations like China won't matter much because we will still have the basics needed to sustain?

Tilling the land will give children physical health and physical life.

Tilling the soil will give education in physical work. This will improve both physical strength and education in mental work so we can have a smart and healthy nation again.

Tilling the soil will also give children education in God's nature and what could be more right for learning?

Tilling the soil will also heal families as families work together for food they eat. Each will learn responsibility again and each will also learn teamwork and family values.

What could be greater than food to eat from the gardens grown on freedom soil?

Plenty to eat is the option which beats the other, and now you know how America can have plenty! It comes from tilling our own soil and not depending upon the other!

P.S. – Progress isn't measured by how America does in the global economy! That's failure! Progress is measured by how we transform our lives by the richest human values, which are also the most traditional values, which have served humanity since the beginning of mankind!

Policy On Global Economy

Policy on global economy starts with having a successful national economy. This is one that serves humanity within our national borders. Marriage, family, children, livelihood, and national economy are all important.

When a nation knows how to care for its own, that nation can contribute to the global economy. A successful global economy happens when a world of nations know how to take care of their own.

Our most valuable export in America can be the knowledge we possess to take care of our own and show other nations how. This way, we can spread freedom and not slavery around the globe.

Make national governments around the world accountable to serve their own people or show their people the right to remake government. This global policy provides proper incentive for nations to be friendly to one another and work in harmony instead of war so all can work together to serve the needs of nations.

End entitlement thinking around the globe by making each national government accountable to serve its own or face consequence by the will of their people.

Teach the world the right of the people to have government of the people, by the people, and for the people or exercise the people's right to replace those in government giving the people slavery.

Empower the people to shape their will and there will be a better globe.

I support having good global partners who operate according to principles of truth and freedom. In the spirit of friendship, I support helping those who are willing to help themselves to live by truthful standards. Those who have no will should plan on living in slavery. Let each nation be shaped by the will and judgment of its people. I support helping as many nations as possible when we can in order to further freedom, but first, we must take care of our own so we can model freedom for the world and not go broke in the process.

I support teaching how to fish rather than giving all of the fish away.

This is a policy on global economy.

The Real Reason For War

If you've wondered what is the real reason for war, here it is.

Wherever you are, others are there with you. The world is a dangerous place. It is your world.

Your world can be shattered at any moment by those who think evil. The world witnessed that on 9-11. On that day and every other day in history, evil has inflicted evil upon the innocent by those who think evil. Evil also continues to ravage innocence every day at every level of humanity.

Unless you overcome evil, evil will overcome you.

This is a message for anti-war protestors. At what point does it become selfish and self-serving when you see evil inflicted on others but you do not care as long as it doesn't affect you? At what point does it not bother you that evil men have wealth to manufacture, buy, and sell weapons of mass destruction for completely evil intentions?

The attack of 9-11 came to innocent people, and to their families, and to all Americans unjustified. How should we respond to evil?

That depends totally upon the enemy. Winning doesn't come from ignoring the enemy. Life is shaped mostly by how we respond to good and evil and timing is critical. Your response to evil should be stronger than the evil that threatens you. If you don't respond first, evil may find you first and that would be a foolish miscalculation on your part.

How about negotiating with evil? Does that work?

Never before in human history has anyone removed the ways of evil from common men. This makes negotiation with evil a game of guesswork. Unless you are the first person in history to figured out how to control evil through negotiation, you would be foolish to think you could. You can try to negotiate with evil but if evil doesn't cooperate, you must be smart enough to draw battle lines before you become the target of evil and the victim of evil.

One only has to look at most fundamental lessons of history to understand the reasons for war. Apparently anti-reality people aren't studying their history books.

Freedom is free only in an anti-reality world. It comes from an artificial world of TV screens, computer monitors, video games, and people who have lost the will to fight for freedom. If all conventional wisdom is correct, people are the product of their learning. What the anti-war people are learning is a world of anti-reality they have come to know from unreal sources.

Jeremiah 2:13 tells us …

My people have committed two evils. They have forsaken me the fountain of living waters, and they have hewed them out cisterns, broken cisterns that can hold no water.

When artificial reality is the way of the day more than the reality of God and His instruction book for life, consequences come in the way of wrong priorities, wrong ways to think, live, and choose. Then, failure ensues with all forms of slavery.

One way is the path of failure and the other is the path of success.

One patriot said - "War is an ugly thing. Only one thing is uglier … when people have lost the will to fight for freedom!"

Freedom isn't free! This is the real reason for war.

Keep Freedom For Children

For children, keep freedom and walls of the home.

Freedom for children happens by keeping walls of the home. Walls of the home stand straight, strong, and true. They tell all who see that family live within these walls. Walls also protect family from intruders and winds of bad weather.

Walls of the home aren't just for watching football. They also give us lessons from sports which tell us how to win freedom by standing together.

To keep freedom for children, all of us should be like walls of the home. We should stand straight, strong, and true together when the reasons for freedom show. Others will see our strength. They in turn, will want the same for children.

Show others why we are here. We are here to keep freedom for children. Let's give our best so children will have freedom. This includes ending corruption in government to keep freedom for children. It also includes new economic policies for prospering children.

As I see it, we have two choices. We will either stand up for freedom or sit down and let Chinese economics and exploitation by the few run all over us!

America's Power To Influence: An Anti-terror Message

All seeking power to influence should look at this. It is histories most potent lesson regarding power to influence. This message also applies to America as a nation and all who represent America in leadership roles politically and in every other practical way.

One solitary life –

A man was born in an obscure village, the child of a peasant woman. He grew up in another obscure village. He worked in a carpenter shop until he was 30 and then for a short period of time he was an itinerant preacher. He never went to college. He never had a family. He never owned a home. He never held an office. He never wrote a book. He never traveled 200 miles from the place where he was born. He never did one of the things that usually accompany greatness. He had no credentials but himself. While still a young man the tide of popular religious opinion turned against him. His friends ran away. One of them denied him. Another betrayed him. He was turned over to his religious enemies. He went through the mockery of a trial. He was nailed to a cross in the midst of two malefactors and two robbers. While he was dying, his executioners gambled for the only piece of property that he had on earth - his seamless robe. When he was dead he was laid in a borrowed grave.

Nineteen centuries have come and gone, and today he is the centerpiece of the human race and the leader of all the columns of progress. I am far within the mark when I say that of all the armies that every marched, all the navies ever built, all the parliaments that ever sat, all the kings that ever reigned, and all the presidents that every ruled, plus all the men and women of power who have ever lived, put together have not affected the life of man upon this earth as powerfully as have that one solitary life, Jesus Christ of Nazareth, the man of Galilee. - Author unknown.

P.S. - Here is the key to power and influence - follow him and seek, live, and speak the truth he spoke. Our greatest possession is the land between the ears and in the heart. He said, "The kingdom of God is within you". It is not about carnal land but rather spiritual. This is the only land that can make every soul happy and complete!

One Nation, Under God, Indivisible ...

So often, I have wanted to express the meaning of one nation, under God, indivisible in a way I have come to know which has never been told. Here it is.

One nation is unmatched in strength because the people of one nation are united with one heart and one mind around most compelling truth. Truth always works and nothing works better for building unity in a nation!

Under God is the way to have unity because God says everything best with standards that are perfect and perfectly compelling like no other can say it. Truth is not religion or any other man-made ideology. It is the answers of life from God to man. Truth provides all of the answers and works to bring success of the richest kind to every realm and to every purpose under heaven. His ways give understanding, convictions, beliefs, and values to a nation.

Indivisible means undivided because all who know truth have purpose to stand together in one standard of unity! This standard makes sense like no other for maximum success and freedom for individual, family, business, and country. Undivided because no outcome could be greater than that which comes from truth! Nothing could be greater than standing together as one to enjoy all of the best together as one nation undivided in ways which make us whole.

America is indivisible in our problems and in our blessings. When some have problems, we all do. When some have blessings, we all do. We must think like one nation undivided in both our problems and blessings so we can work together as one to make all things better.

Currently, there is too much partisan politics in government and truth is needed to save us from it. Save America with truth and bring America back from slavery to freedom. It also means repeating the same together to achieve the task. Every person can make a difference.

Partisan politics isn't working! Also, there are far too many opinions. A way without truth is lost in opinions. Have you heard the truth about opinions? Everyone has one! When a nation doesn't have truth, everyone has an opinion which means every one is so right and every one else is so wrong! Then, no one can work together because everyone is so right and every other is so wrong.

The answer to ending partisan politics is truth. Truth answers every question with most brilliant answers, values, and beliefs. Truth works for all and benefits all like no other. Truth also makes more sense than any opinion so there can be less opinions floating around.

You can't have unity when your opinions only work for you and not others.

Violating other's individual rights is also no way to have unity.

Nor can there be unity by abusing others.

Truth is the answer for enjoying a logical game plan, top results, and freedom by doing things right. This is the knowledge from God. It contains all of the answers, the greatest common sense, and the ways which work best for one and all. See the chapter in this book about how to know what is truth.

I support one nation, under God, indivisible with liberty and justice for all! This is the way to save America!

Separation Of Church And State

The original intent of law by America's first lawmakers set the precedent for separation of church and state. This is the answer like nothing in public domain. This message gives the answer like nothing you've seen.

Separation of church and state wasn't about protection FROM religion as some ignorantly teach. Neither was it to protect the feelings of reprobates who find offence at the very thought of God. Separation of church and state is an issue too often misinterpreted by misguided judges who appease reprobates. This is not the reason for separation of church and state.

Separation of church and state came to America by the forefathers of America who came from a tyrannical government in Europe. In Europe, it was common for the pope and the king to join as financial partners in crime. For each sin committed by the common people, the pope and king required financial penance (payment) for sins committed. This partnership capitalizing on the "sins" of the people was profitable.

America's forefathers came to America primarily to regain religious freedom. This freedom would enable them once again to enjoy lifestyle based on authentic praiseworthy values of God.

This freedom was to include freedom from the previous tyrannical practices of both government and denominational religion. To do so, they needed to separate the powers of denominational religion from government. This is how separation of church and state was born.

Today, the common practice of separation of church and state is tyranny. Tyranny is also opposite to freedom because it hinders how people believe, live, and express them selves freely.

The opposite of truth is error and error doesn't work. Error is sheer stupidity. Error is responsible for complete slavery when failure is repeated over and over again. This is why America is facing slavery. In order for America to remain free, our judges must stop interpreting laws to accommodate reprobates. Instead, there must be a return to the truth about the separation of church and state for victory answers.

Separation of church and state was never intended to remove God from government or any part of life. It was meant to do the opposite - protect basic freedom so individuals can believe and express what they want spiritually without reprisal.

One religion dare not violate the rights of another religion. That violates the fundamentals of spiritual love and respect for others and robs one's religion the power to win others from other religions. Violation of people's rights is also the reason for partisan politics.

America's forefathers were men who had honor for God. This honor led them to know Biblical truth and then write the U.S. Constitution. The U.S. Constitution, like no other secular document, respects freedom. Where do you stand regarding freedom?

You shall know the truth and the truth shall make you free!

I support separation of church and state in order to guarantee freedom of speech, freedom of religion, and freedom to live as one chooses without violating others and without being violated by government or religion.

P.S. - Concerning freedom of speech, I support the right to publicly praise all things of value. Those who are critics of freedom of speech have nothing to offer of value. Freedom of speech works to determine the difference! Freedom of speech and religion is a nation's way to find something of value. It comes with self-expression. All with something positive to say should say it. All of the rest, the critics, should be quiet or risk exposing their ignorant ideas which have no value. A nation without freedom of speech is a nation without values.

Regarding "ten commandments" and other ornaments of faith in public places, I support leaving those in place. They are part of America's history as signs to show the world how the greatest nation was built. This is a part of history and no one has a right to steal America's history! I support using good judgment on future ornamental displays based on individual political location. I support respecting the religious views of others before putting more religious ornaments in public use. That doesn't say I wouldn't. I support separation of church and state according to history's definition. This includes the right to reference God and religion in any public forum.

Right To Die

Right to die is God given just like other rights. See in this message how God doesn't manipulate people in this right like those do in their man-made religious ways. This message clarifies how God gives rights. This includes right to die.

God's grace is what gives the right to make individual choices concerning all most significant topics starting at the top with eternal life. God gives choice even in that and He doesn't lose His state of love with that choice. That choice is in Romans 10:9 which you can look up.

God's grace also applies to everything lesser including physical life. New Testament times are all about grace and not law. If God wanted law to ban right to die and all choices surrounding it, He would have replaced New Testament grace with law.

God loves even in right to die. Romans 8:37 & 38 reads ...

For I am persuaded that neither death, nor life, nor angels, nor principalities, nor powers, nor things to come, nor height, nor depth, nor any other creature, shall be able to separate us from the love of God, which is in Christ Jesus our Lord.

Current laws restricting right to die also victimize individuals in their right to choose. These laws also fail God's standard of grace in the Bible as well as His message of grace.

How do they victimize? One most obvious way is by mandating extra human suffering on those who die with extended painful death because options given by God are made illegal by laws of men.

Those who miss God's message of grace and mercy are also missing His message of love!

The truth of God in the Bible always keeps us in our best frame of mind with love and respect and not legalism, for others. When we exceed his doctrine with man-made legalism, some get hurt.

The right to die physically in modest comfort and dignity is graciously extended to every other life form. Even pets are granted the courtesy of dying HUMANELY! Some of those among the religious element miss this whole message. The results are insensitive, cruel, and opposite to the grace and love of God.

All have a right to die without unnecessary human suffering and with loving acceptance and support from those who care most. Wouldn't you also want this?

Politicians and judges, keep your religious laws off of individual rights. That is where separation of church and state applies. This is how there can be more unconditional Christian love and respect for others in the right to choose.

I support love and respect for others in the personal choice to end extreme pain and suffering! I would have to question the character of others who oppose this view!

P.S. - Error works for some. Truth works for all!

Stem Cell Research

This message shows God's perspective, a spiritual look at stem cell research.

There are two kinds of life, physical and spiritual.

Physical life doesn't have the same priority as spiritual life in God's book.

I John 5:12 *He that hath the Son hath life: and he that hath not the Son of God hath not life.*

Stems cells are not spiritual. Neither are they soul life according to God' description in Genesis 2:7.

And the Lord God formed man of the dust of the ground, and breathed into his nostrils the breath of life: and man became a living soul.

Any definition other than this fails to recognize God definition.

In order to be wise to the spiritual, it is helpful to separate the difference between spiritual and physical. Physical priorities obviously don't deserve the same treatment. God doesn't want us warring after the flesh when we have more important things to do.

Some give equal respect to physical life as they do to spiritual life. Consider how carnally wrong this is. Consider how humans do worse acts than animals! That isn't good and that certainly isn't spiritual no more than stem cells are spiritual.

Physical life can be bad or good. It is mostly what we do with it.

Genesis tells us that man is dust and unto dust he shall return. Physical life should be respected for what it is. It is made from dust! This is spiritual perspective regarding physical life. God doesn't entangle himself with physical priorities. I believe He would rather see Christians known far and wide for their kind and unconditional love along with their zeal for eternity rather than win the vote to ban stem cell research.

God would have to re-write His book to eliminate the grace in stem cell research. This is after all, a labor of love in the field of physical science to help the living and the good. For this, a ban on stem cell research would be a lost opportunity in the exercise of love.

This is my position on stem cells. Stem cells are not spiritual. Nor do they have the equivalence of human soul life as defined in Genesis 2:7. Stem cells will not win anyone spiritually but the spiritual message of salvation will. Abuse of other's rights who want to pursue better health through stem cell research is a violation of their rights. Any success by Christians to ban stem cell research will work in opposite to respect for the Christian name. Success to ban stem cell research would grow resentment for the Christian way. The Bible says we are not to war after the flesh and I believe this topic does. We don't need more partisan politics in America. We need less if we want to keep freedom and play like a team to solve our real huge problems! Stem cell research is not one of them. I suggest moving on to bigger and better subjects like saving our country and eternal salvation. Also pray that someone comes up with a cure for your disease from their work in stem cell research. I support stem cell research for the good of the living.

The Abortion Debate: How Both Sides Can Win!

The abortion debate has eluded top religious and political leaders for decades. This message reveals the answer to the greatest debate of modern times. The answer is simple, profound, and right from the Bible. The answer helps both sides to win!

Teach how every right choice is built on a solid foundation. When the foundation is right, everything upon that foundation is also right including the issue of childbirth. The foundation is Jesus Christ. When he is taught right, all other issues are solved. Correct ways give priority to the spiritual over the physical.

His message provides perfect ways to live in wholeness and shape attitude correctly so the abortion debate is settled even before it begins. Obviously, Christian people have lost their footing and foundation. The abortion debate has turned from spiritual to physical and no one is winning.

I believe physical life is mortal and spiritual life is eternal. I believe abortion is a physical issue rather than spiritual and therefore, needs to be managed by physical standards. I believe physical life can be bad or good. The difference is determined by what we do with it. The results can also be bad or good. This includes the issue of pregnancy and every other issue affecting the life of a baby after birth. This also includes the life of a would-be mother. There are many more choices after birth rather than before.

I support managing every decision relating to pregnancy so every decision after that serves both physical and spiritual priorities. I believe not all do. I believe those decisions which do not serve the greater good are wrong.

Romans 8:6 - *For to be carnally minded is death (spiritual failure) but to be spiritually minded is life and peace.*

I believe some pregnancy starts with slam, bam, thank you ma'am, and that is not spiritual. As a result, not all births serve right priorities in either physical or spiritual.

For more on physical and spiritual life and the difference, see "Stem cell research" in this book. This topic also clarifies from Biblical view when cells become souls.

The greatest solution to ending abortion happens by winning hearts and minds spiritually and intellectually so more individuals make smarter sexual choices. This will reduce the need for abortion.

The second solution is the answer to failing the first answer. The second answer involves separation of church and state and individual right to choose. I support the right to choose so physical and spiritual priorities are both managed rather than slam, bam, thank you ma'am!

I believe pro-life is a misnomer name and a misrepresentation of God. I believe pro-life has lost its way by supporting slam, bam, thank you ma'am and turning wrong decisions into slaves. Slavery comes from the wrong end of life. I believe the Christian way should be serving the spiritual side so all children born are born with love and service spiritually.

Too many children today are born unwanted, unloved, and abused because they originate from the physical seeds of irresponsibility and slavery rather than spiritual seeds of love.

I don't believe in the name or integrity of pro-life because the name politically disparages the spiritual goodness of God in others.

I don't believe in trading spirituality for carnal subjects like the pro-life movement is doing.

I do believe in winning souls to Christ! This is how both sides of the abortion debate can win!

P.S. – Christians have much larger concerns than abortion. Because they have been in the dark so long with less than spiritual priorities, communist China's ideology is threatening all of Christianity, all of America, and all of religious freedom!

Sex, Family, And Freedom: The Other Side Of Homosexuality

This message describes sexuality from a broad view in order to draw a most positive conclusion about the parts that fit together as a whole.

Good sex benefits society as a whole. It also benefits every realm of life. With all that is gained through good sex, it has power to lift a nation to greatest success, success contributing to continued freedom.

There is also a long list of consequences for using it the opposite way. This includes failure of relationships at the very foundation of society. This includes failure as individual, male, female, family, child, and more! This message clarifies good sex and opposite sex and how to differentiate so all can choose wisely and keep freedom.

Opposite sex is homosexuality.

This message clarifies the impact of good sex versus homosexuality on the future of America. You will see how good sex benefits humanity from child-hood to the grave. Homosexuality reaps havoc from child-hood to the grave.

Good sex helps America to live in success and remain free. Heed this message or suffer the consequence for non-compliance. The consequence of misuse is failure, then, the consequence of failure is slavery. Failure and slavery happen when parts of society fail to perform right.

The fruit of each can show the difference between right and wrong. Right produces benefits. Wrong produces consequences.

Jesus Christ said, *For a good tree bringeth not forth corrupt fruit: neither doth a corrupt tree bring forth good fruit.* - Luke 7:43

You can tell if sex is used right by the impact it has on family life. The right way supports family life. The wrong way harms it.

America is not invincible to harm. When the family unit is harmed, a list of consequences occurs. These consequences are dangerous to America's future. Why? Because, as the family goes, so goes the nation!

Clearly, the nation's morality is growing weaker. This destructive direction will continue unless traditional values are taught, embraced, and improved.

Two trains of thought fuel the good sex versus homosexuality debate. The gene theory is most responsible for homosexual acceptance. This is not science, only a theory! This theory assumes sexual orientation is determined genetically. This view rejects traditional ideas that good sexuality can be shaped by values, education, and environment. Therefore, those who accept the gene theory will have no reason to even consider shaping sexuality a better way built on good values, education, or environmental factors.

Traditional view considers all of the above to be useful, important, and empowering.

Since the gene theory rejects all of the above as means to contribute to sexuality, it also includes a message of hopelessness, despair, and defeat. The traditional view is performance based. It is also incentive based and embraces every opportunity of encouragement, insight, reason, education, and more to produce right choices and positive steps forward to shape sex life by traditional values. Which do you prefer, the hopeless way or the way to improve to serve traditional values?

Here is more regarding both ways. First, the performance way -
· We are what we choose to think about
· We are what we choose to look at
· We are what we choose to talk about
· We are what we choose to believe
· We are what we choose to promote

• We are the result of the environment we choose to surround ourselves with

• We are influenced by and become like the people we choose to be with

• We are better to believe truth and align our lives with Biblical truth rather than travel new trails of homosexual acceptance like the media is promoting. Will we promote the doctrine of God or choose the media message instead with new and devastating kinds of doctrine never seen before on large scale?

Freedom in the sexual realm is just like freedom in every realm. Freedom isn't free. It takes desire, focus, and discipline to shape everything the right way.

Some are deceived like the gardener taught to neglect the garden while the weeds over-run the garden.

Consider the following to be a part of good sex – dad, mom, family, brothers, sisters, and whole relationships between males and females.

Obviously, the anatomy difference between male and female is a perfect compliment between two. But the benefits also go much deeper. The difference is also obvious in emotional make-up of males and females. The two are different, but by working together, they compliment one another!

The following are benefits of good sex. None of these are available to homosexuals.

• Marriage to the opposite sex as an attractive sex difference! This difference compliments each other!
• Marriage to the opposite sex as a complimentary companion for life!
• Marriage to the opposite sex as a compliment in child rearing and parenting!
• Marriage to the opposite sex as a compliment in emotions, reason, and counsel!

Notice how each of these is a compliment without deadly consequences to society. Also notice how non-compliance to any of these voids the benefits. Without the benefits of good sex, failure and slavery ensue.

Good sex also benefits the needs of children because it benefits the relationships of parents. Children need to be accepted and loved deeply by the age old, timeless standard of mother and father. Little boys need acceptance and love by both parents as little boys and little girls need acceptance and love by both parents as little girls. Homosexuality can't do either!

· Acceptance and love from both parents shapes positive self-esteem and self-identity which little boys and little girls need from mommies and daddies in order to develop positive self-esteem.

· This identity will be the blue print for a lifetime for these little ones.
· This will also be the basis for their relationships with people of both sexes.
· This will also be the basis for understanding the difference between the sexes.
· This is also the basis for how to be successful in relationships with both sexes
· Children will carry this identity into everything they do and with every relationship they have.
· It's about being a successful person as either male or female.

America the beautiful, this message underscores the need for successful relationships between males and females at every level of culture! These relationships can be built upon a common understanding of males and females and how they work together as compliments to each other.
There are no better lessons for males and females than those learned from each other in intimacy. These lessons play out in other very practical society ways. These are the same lessons homosexuals cannot know or teach.

The rest of this message is straight from the Bible.

The original plan for sex came from Genesis. It is about the man and woman becoming one flesh together in marriage.

The man and woman in marriage are to be helpmates. Also, the man is to be to the woman as Christ is to the church while the woman is to be to the man as the church is to Christ.

This is God's plan for marriage for top personal fulfillment!

It is a message about sex between male and female. Homosexuality does not and cannot partake in these benefits. Therefore, homosexuality fails at all of them.

See how every point above makes perfect sense. See how every opposing way cancels the benefits. See how non-compliance is the perfect path to failure. Failure doesn't work! It only leads to slavery!

Jesus Christ said, *He that is not with me is against me: and he that gathers not with me scattereth.*

America, the beautiful! Will you stand united with a potent message or will your voice be smothered by the voice of ignorance? Will you sow discord among brethren because you don't stand united? Whether you stand or fall, your decision will be felt by all Americans, little and great! The result will either be freedom or slavery! United we stand on truth or divided we fall!

Sex affects every level of life and culture. Good sex and the benefits of good sex are reasons to embrace these standards for the improvement of culture. Success won't happen by staring in space. It starts by reading your Bible and learning how to live more successfully.

Homosexuality is a lost cause and a school in hopelessness, futility, defeat, and failure. It is everything opposite to family and since family is the foundation to society, homosexuality is everything opposite including failure of society and slavery! Please pray for those who desire traditional values alive and well in their sex life.

And ye shall know the truth and the truth shall make you free - John 8:32.

This is a perfect position for sex and freedom!

P.S. – Politicians supporting homosexuality are bottom feeders looking for more votes!

Fund Either Homosexual Values Or Family Values

The choice is one or the other. There is only so much money for benefits.

If you've ever had questions about morality, funding homosexual partner benefits is taking food off of the table for the timeless institution of family and family values! This is dad, mom, and kids if anyone happened to forget.

I put family values first! I support funding family values, not homosexual unions.

Also, I would like to see more health care benefit go to those who contribute to society and less to those who don't (i.e. - criminals).

America's ten dumbest deeds starting with #10

10. Buying gas for the most impressive gas-guzzlers from terrorists bent on destroying America!

9. Raising children on day cares, TV screens, and computer monitors instead of dad, mom, and the family love!

8. Rather than the ounce of prevention worth a pound of cure with products made for health, junk food continues to be the purchase of choice for creating the worst economic nightmare!

7. Buying products supporting the wishes of communist leader's to own America and turn America's consumers into slaves!

6. Rather than starting children at five years old to work physically and think mentally, parents are waiting until their children reach age eighteen after the thinking process is mostly lost!

5. Raising the minimum wage on the low end without taxing more the high end. This will simply raise the pricing on everything anyway and continue the imbalance even more!

4. Rather than protecting America's majority power-base, the few in Washington are grabbing the power which will then be stripped from them by the largest power grabber of all, communist China!

3. Rather than working together to solve the nations largest problems, many are choosing to do nothing at all while every part of their quality of life sinks below sea level!

2. Having a president selling no new taxes while at the same time, he is selling off our jobs!

1. The 300 million-majority can't form enough majority to tell less than six hundred souls in Washington what to do! The Great Majority Power Move is the way to do it!

How To End Treason In Government

The Intro

Certain elected officials need to be reminded of our laws which protect America from treason so they start serving sovereign interests rather than corporate interests and foreign interests. Some of them have bought into the new global economy and a new world order. This new ideology is selling off our sovereign interests, our children, our families, our livelihoods, and our national economy, to corporate interests and foreign interests.

They are buying into the wrong offer. Ego, greed, and desire to exploit the majority are threatening America's very existence including U.S. ability to protect from the worst adversaries.

A small group of politicians in Washington actively pursuing the trade corridor with Canada and Mexico are thick in the plot! Their actions are beyond stupid. Instead, they are taking deliberate steps to dismantle sovereignty by their crimes of treason.

Protection from treason is how to save America from treasonous acts. The following contains the plan!

Grounds For Treason

Elected officials voting against the majority and against the constitution which protects the sovereign interests of the majority, are candidates for treason. These elected officials took an oath of public trust to uphold the Constitution. Instead, they are trading it to corporate interests and foreign interests for personal gain as if America's human treasures are worth no more than a business deal! There is a corporate take-over of our country happening right now due to their corruption!

The time has come to reclaim the function and integrity of our government and the U.S. Constitution as it applies to the U.S. economy. If we don't, our families and freedom's children all over America will pay the highest price for our lack of action. The voting records of elected officials makes it obvious that some are not serving the interests of America's human treasures and they are not serving the sovereign interests of the U.S. Constitution.

America's laws protect America's human treasures from the few who would sell off the sovereign interests of America to foreign interests. That would be a breach of public trust and that is treason!

Numbers are tangible measures to determine the practice of treason. Figures don't lie by liars figure. It is easy to tell when treason occurs when illegal immigrants receive more benefits than U.S. born citizens. It is easy to tell when corporate interests are served better and more often than interests of the human majority. It is easy to tell when voting records of politicians do not enforce the laws on the books which make illegal immigration illegal. America was made a people's republic and a people's state, not a corporate state, and protecting the people's state is a most basic function of the U.S. Constitution.

The people of this nation must grasp what treason is if they are to deserve its protection. Neither will they have protection unless they demand enforcement of law as it applies to treason. Just as most problems in America today come from treason, most of our solutions will come from enforcing the laws of treason. Enforcement of law will bring back order and priority. Correct order serves the American people rather than a new world order where there are no rules of order to manage good over evil.

Why should we be looking to enforce the laws of treason for rogue politicians who have strayed from their entrusted sovereign duties? Much is at stake! Currently, because of treasonous acts, America's majority is being led down a very real and progressive path of economic enslavement and other forms of enslavement to the lead of communist China's low price and other low wages of $2.00 per day around the globe. The cost of communist economics is by itself enough to enslave any people of any nation forced to compete with such low wage exploitation. This is all happening because our politicians have not been serving the sovereign interests of their own country. Instead, they have been serving their political careers and the lobby groups paying their way.

This is more about treason and why those who commit treason should be held accountable. This is also the answer to cleaning up our political system FAST from corruption threatening America's very existence. This is also about renewing America's strength as a sovereign nation to serve the majority, America's human treasures, rather than selling off the people of America to the highest and lowest bidder!

Solution To Ending Treason

Draw public attention to this outrage! Heighten public awareness to the large problem of treason. This is America's WORST problem! Awaken the majority by sharing this book. Also, follow the steps of the Great Majority Power Move to alert others! Everyone doing a little will make the largest difference. Also, this cause will spread by public media! Also, wear the "Talk of Treason" message shirt which promotes the message. Hundreds and thousands can view it. This shirt will mean much more to your freedom than any other. Other apparel has no message and no solution! With enough public out-cry, Washington will change! "Talk of Treason" can be purchased at: www.USAFreedom.us. Our life in America is for sale and the treasonous sale must be stopped! End this problem for America's largest national solution!

P.S. – In order to change America, America must be reached tangibly and changed visually! Fashions of Free (Talk of Treason and others) make it easy to reach very large crowds with a remarkable spectacle. One shirt can be viewed by thousands! Many shirts can change the nation! If you don't spend $20.00, you won't have a country!

Talk Of Revolution

Right to revolution is found in America's Declaration of Independence. It is more than just legal. It is a legitimate obligation of leadership in government of the people!

It states … *"When in the Course of human Events, it becomes necessary for one People to dissolve the political Bands which have connected them with another, and to assume among the Powers of the Earth, the separate and equal Station to which the Laws of Nature and of Nature's God entitle them, a decent Respect to the Opinions of Mankind requires that they should declare the causes which impel them to the Separation."*

Our duty is to do what is right even when the laws of the land fail to do so. Then, it is our duty to disobey those laws for the sake of higher laws and change those needing change.

America's majority can avoid a bloody revolution and won't need more than a peaceful revolution if galvanized with a right mind-set. The majority must refuse to be oppressed and raped by the few. The few also need to know that their ways of economic rape, extortion, and treason will not be tolerated. Mind-sets need to change and relationships need to change.

Political leaders, judges, corporate executives, doctors, dentists, and more should not be abusive to America's human treasures! What is worse, sexual rape or economic rape? Both are punishable by the highest law and America needs that protection from the worst offenders!

P.S. - How will you know when revolution is in order? Play the game according to the demand to win. Economic rape, extortion, and treason will not be tolerated!

Talk of Revolution is the answer to cleaning up abuse by the few!

P.P.S. – Galvanize the will of the 300 million-majority to no longer accept the lies and deception of the few selling the majority to economic slavery. Protect the future by promoting this message. Buy the "Talk of Revolution" shirt for hundreds, thousands, and millions to view it. Buy it at: www.USAFreedom.us

Because freedom is so important to our future, revolution is always a Constitutional right and God-given right in order to change WHATEVER needs changing to keep freedom! There's plenty of talent in 300 million to do it! Unified effort by the majority can make it extremely simple and extremely attainable! 500,000 Americans to every one politician is ripe condition for change! Revolution can be peaceful and fun.

Ripe For Revolution

With 536 failed politicians selling the people's state of 300 million to a corporate state, a foreign state, and a communist state against your will, conditions are ripe for revolution. We'd be stupider than stupid not to think so since remaining idle would be like standing in the middle of the road while a semi-truck is coming down the road.

The semi is communist economics. When the bulk of our consumer goods are made by people earning $2.00 per day, that will ruin you! The few in Washington are doing something extremely stupid. They are transferring the power of the majority to the few so communist China's military might will find it easy to transfer the power from the few! Currently, all of the economic and military power is going to China.

300 million have the power to take back America the Beautiful from 536 failed politicians. The ratio is 500,000 to every one failed politician. We'd be a bunch of girly men if we didn't win this one! The answer is not 300 million divided parts. We have that now and that is failure! The answer is 300 million as one! This book reveals how.

Apathy, indifference, and defeat are not tolerable! They are certainly not American either! Those who don't love America and don't do what it takes to take care of it, should leave! They don't deserve a country anyway! If the great majority doesn't' stand together, you won't have a country!

All good causes you support are worth nothing if you don't support this cause to save the nation of your dreams and all you value within it! I am giving 300 million American's the power to take it back by supporting one most important cause – saving your nation!

My book contains America's only real game plan for taking it back! Every freedom loving American should own a copy of this book so you can practice being an American again! Your other option is to continue the current path leading to America's worst nightmare and the ultimate failure from your failure to act!

P.S. – We don't need a bloody revolution. It can be a peaceful and fun revolution if we the people repeat the same simple deeds and one most potent voice together, beyond 536 failed politicians. The details are in this book only if you care for what happens to the future of freedom's children!

The Greatest Words Ever Recorded For Unifying A Nation

Unity happens very different from partisan politics in Washington. Obviously, the current exchange of tit for tat isn't working. Unity happens when America's great majority has purpose to repeat the same deed together for better quality of life and a better future. Then there can be unity! This is that message for restoring the greatest nation with solid improvements!

Partisan politics is no longer tolerable. United we stand! Divided we fall! To end corporate exploitation and communist economics, a common goal is needed!

Unity is required in order to save the greatest nation from the worst nightmare to come. The worst nightmare includes the progressive advancement of corporate exploitation and communist economics. All politicians who continue partisan politics should resign from office or be "fired" for repeating failure! One small group is also eligible for treason! This kind of failure only facilitates more of the same. Please note, rampant poverty will ABSOLUTELY occur UNLESS corporate exploitation and communist economics are REPLACED with traditional policy! If both continue, they will be the reason for America's worst nightmare. Both can be conquered with a winning message like this one in this book! Both can be conquered with this winning game plan!

Unity happens with universal answers which work for all. Only one source provides such intellect! That is the author of all richest values and insights. That is God Himself, the maker of all success and all life. His message in the Bible is the answer. His answers work for all! The answers in this book are proof of that!

Unity doesn't happen by ignoring His message! Nor does it happen by acting on human intellect much smaller than His. Human intellect is the part failing us now.

Unity has already been completed over two thousand years ago. It was completed by the world savior. He did it by perfecting values for achieving unity.

Unity is now a finished work. Now we can have unity. It doesn't happen by looking for a new standard. It happens by simply repeating the one completed over two thousand years ago. This unity includes the highest thoughts and emotions in human domain for us to think!

The Bible tells us to keep unity. It doesn't tell us to make unity.

Ephesians 4: 2-3 *With all lowliness and meekness, with longsuffering, forbearing one another in love: Endeavoring to keep the unity of the spirit in the bond of peace.*

Unity happens when hearts and minds do what is right for the good of all to keep unity. The answers are opposite to failure! The details are provided in the Bible.

This is our answer to unifying the greatest nation. Leaders who know this answer are the answer to unifying the greatest nation.

These are the greatest words ever recorded for unifying a nation!

Obviously, the leaders in Washington don't have the answer. They are at best Sunday morning Christians who know little about applying this message six other days in the week!

P.S. – 300 million divided can't achieve anything! This is our nation now without a game plan. This book shows the game plan. This book in the hands of millions is the antidote for solving indifference, apathy, and defeat! Millions repeating this same potent message together can improve everything! Helping every good cause other than this one won't help either if you lose your country!

The next section, How to prosper a nation opposite to every failure and expense, will add more to this message of unity!

How To Prosper A Nation Opposite To Every Failure And Expense!

There is great cost savings for all Americans and much improved economic future by doing something easy and different. All of the best occurs by going opposite to every great failure and expense. The results also have huge impact on all parts of America's future – more money available for education of children, more money to cover health care costs, environmental issues, military defense, and every prosperous way imaginable by saving the largest costs! The remainder of this book is dedicated to doing just that. These answers are also found on the LifeStylers USA website, a Mark Dean original about success coaching. See it at: www.LifeStylersUSA.com.

Saving Health / Saving Health Care Costs

With such high costs for health care, saving these costs has become a number one concern for Americans everywhere. And since so much illness is preventable, this topic offers a remarkable place to start for saving the largest costs!

These costs are expensive now and by current trends, they will climb much higher. Some experts estimate that health care costs will double in the next ten years. What is the answer?

What could affect health more than products consumed in the body daily?

For the largest cost savings, look first at the products going into the body every day! Most are made with little thought for saving health. In fact, many do just the opposite. The obvious choice is just the opposite. Build health care savings on products made for health. These also offer other most remarkable benefits – looking good, feeling good, and living a long time. What would fifteen additional happy healthy years mean to you? What would it mean to your family? What would it mean to your pocket book to dodge one or two major diseases and all health care costs that go with it? Would this be worth special focus? The answers are simple!

The LifeStylers USA approach to saving health care costs has two-parts; daily consumables from the world leader in health and nutrition plus coaching to gain teamwork, timing, rhythm, and momentum to win your greatest wins in health just like star athletes win in sports.

For more about saving health and health care costs, go to: ww.LifeStylersUSA.com!

About Children

All Things Are Possible

What children learn can be a life changing difference for them. They can either learn a life of success or a life of failure, the life of a prince or the life of a pauper. The following are ideas for bringing a life of success to the world of children where all things are possible!

On Child Bonding

Remember when children were raised on the farm?

Life was simple then. The world children knew was also simple. It was a world of family. Families lived together, worked together, and played together. They did much together.

Full time relationships also brought full time bonding. This bonding was simple, focused, and uncluttered.

Today, the bond is broken. Parents are not living with their children like they did back then. And images of life are not coming from family and the real life experience they gained on the farm.

Instead, today's images are muddied. Parents are away from home working. And children are spending much more time at day care, and on TV screens and computer monitors, and around nasty, abused children that nice children meet in school.

Is it any wonder why families are no longer the same?

The images children receive today are many and separate from parents and family and positive real life themes.

Is there fun, laughter, and joy in families? The answer is simple! Only if we make it happen by spending much time together!

Families can come back to the reality of living together. They can by working together, playing together, and living together at home with the help of a family run business right at home. Here children can learn about livelihood and they can learn how to live.

The Influence Of TV On Children

One could hardly consider the welfare of children without also considering what they watch. What they watch is about eleven hours of TV per week.

The following is a candid look at what is happening to a nation of children. Your question, "Do I want a nation of children (mine and others) to be a part of this crowd and how can I fix it?"

Eleven hours of TV represents eleven hours of prime time in a little life and prime time for bonding. What are children bonding to? One thing is for certain. They are not bonding to parents and family or anything real! What they are bonding to at best, are cartoon heroes which talk like humans.

What children are bonding to is a false reality they cannot trust. Since when are cartoons real? And since when do animals talk like humans? Cartoon makers are loading up artificial cartoon figures with human emotions and human appeal.

Perhaps even you have been influenced without even realizing it, a world of deception which takes you out of reality and into a world of false priorities. One thing leads to another and first thing you know, there is a whole new culture never seen before in human history; an anti-reality culture based on cartoon heroes and animals which think and talk like people. Have we become more civilized or more deceived?

Has the cartoon world brought people to a new way of thinking, a new reality which takes their emotions for a train ride and drops them off in world of disaster?

There is another option. Teach children how to know life for what it really is. This way, they will have a belief system they can trust to be effective in real life situations.

The Influence of Day Care On Children

Day Care - An economic solution for working parents. The following is the other side of the coin with reason to achieve a better way for children and parents so both can win all across the nation.

All throughout the history of mankind, children have been raised with parents and siblings in the first five forming years of life when bonding is vital to self-identity and self-esteem.

In addition, love and trust bonds are built during this time. These bonds are the basis for other relationships throughout life.

These values children learn have traditionally been shaped most from quality family love from parents and siblings who share life with these little ones.

What is becoming of a nation of children who seem to not have values? How about looking to improve the first five forming years!

What children learn at daycare when mom and dad are away is a world of strangers, children babysitting children; workers making minimum wage and working mostly for money; neglected, abused, nasty children that nice children meet in school; a world of strangers, too many and too strange for little ones to bond to, resulting in a world of insecurity and mistrust.

One way to benefit a nation's families so little ones can be with parents in the ultimate love environment is to show parents how to work from home in a home based business.

LifeStylers USA is one of those for bringing this message to the nation and many others for highly successful living.

Expanding Children's Imagination And Brain Power

Use it or lose it, a few short words regarding the power of children's imagination and brainpower.

The first five years are the forming years for life.

The first five years are critical for growing imagination and brainpower. One common way children are losing imagination and brainpower has to do with the drive-up window way of already prepared images; images they get from TV which requires no self-initiative.

Consider another world where children turn boxes into homes, broom sticks into horses, and beach sand into castles; children who start with nothing and build an empire!

This message is a reminder to parents to help children be children and let them develop something out of nothing with coaching and play with mom and dad.

Images Made For Children

Winning for children is easy with positive mind images. For children, the images in the mind determine most their future. The following is about images of fantasy or images of truth children will come to know. Stories these images produce influence them, their future, and all they do. Today's parents have an opportunity to shape destiny for children based on truth. Here is how.

Give children images of real people doing real good. Not fantasy characters they see on TV which talk like humans and portray unreal images. Real good is not about elves, Easter bunnies, or artificial figures. It is about real life lessons and real life heroes our children can know and become.

Here is one place to start. Read children Bible stories about real people who have overcome obstacles in real ways. Teach them truth from the Bible, persistence, caring, and other good qualities. Also share real life stories about every day heroes who overcome evil with good. Give our children real images they can trust and become.

These are images made for children!

The Link Between Children & Nobel Prize Winners

Did you know there is a common link among Nobel Peace Prize Winners? As children, they are raised around animals and nature?

What do you suppose these children see? Do they see that nature is bigger than they are, sometimes kind and sometimes cruel? Do they see the difference between good and evil and take appropriate steps to protect themselves when needed? Do they see that nature is a teacher with lessons to teach regardless of their mood? Do they see they must pay attention or face nature naturally? Does this teach them how to be more attentive and better students? Does it teach them to learn without a single spoken word? Do they sharpen their skills for learning by engaging all of the five senses; taste, touch, smell, hearing, and sight? Do they learn to engage themselves wholly in the lessons all around them? Do they learn to listen to the silence on a moonlit night? And do they learn to listen to their thoughts and hearts when everything else is quiet? Do they learn to think in natural awesome respect?

These are thoughts for shaping children - lessons for the heart equal to their maker!

Leaders And Followers

Another lesson gained from the farm was the lesson of leaders and followers.

Back then children learned naturally that parents were superior in wisdom and knowledge. Remember, they lived with their parents. These little ones worked with and played with their leaders. Here, parent's experience and leadership was easy to see and easy to follow.

What happens when parents lead with strength as leaders? Children learn to follow and when they do, they grow up to be leaders because they know how to follow.

This lesson is about leaders and followers. When leaders are leaders, they provide the means for others to follow. No one can follow until someone leads with something worthy to follow. And leaders make it happen!

Leaders make followers and followers make leaders.

Before one can lead, he or she must first follow. Success in life is made up of leaders and followers because it takes both working together for the power of teamwork and working together for higher achievement.

It starts at home with father. He heads the family with strength, responsibility, and wisdom which he gets from his perfect Father. And because he leads, mom finds it easy to follow. Together they work as a pair, each helping the other in love and the leadership of one.

One is easier to follow than two. This is why children do better when parents agree and live in one flesh as described in Biblical detail in marriage.

When parents disagree with no standard for truth, children are in chaos with confusion, insecurity, and anarchy. The result: they are unable to follow, a limitation which can follow them for life!

Where children go as adults depends upon where they start as children. Can they follow? Will they know truth from the Bible which leads to trust? Will truth be a solid foundation for that which is right and give them something worthy to follow? If so, children can grow up as leaders because they know how to follow.

Truth teaches the difference between good and evil and right and wrong. This is how children learn how to trust that which is good and not be deceived. And because they know this, they are able to discern all human elements and be selective to build only upon good. As a result, they will know how to succeed in the most important ways as in marriage and in relationships in work and play and in every important way.

This is a message about leaders and followers and how much a nation's children need parents to lead with truth and give children a lifestyle filled with all good; a way worthy to follow!

Train Children To Be Leaders

Strong decisive parents raise children to be strong decisive leaders. Strong decisive parents understand that children need leadership and oversight. Children raised with this kind of leadership have the greatest opportunity for success in the future.

Here is why. From zero to five years of age, children have little reasoning power. They need training in right behavior. Training gives them confidence to perform right. They need training because they lack mental capacity to make right choices.

Granting children adult-like choices is a common mistake. Young children are not emotionally or mentally equipped to make large choices. When parents give children frequent choices and large choices they are not qualified to make, feelings of inadequacy and insecurity take seed.

At five years of age, the mind starts developing more reasoning power; a perfect time to start nurturing reasoning power to make more choices for themselves; first little choices, then bigger choices as they mature toward adulthood.

This includes allowing them to make wrong choices but not dangerous choices. Let them make some wrong choices for learning. Also, love them unconditionally even in wrong choices. Show them they are loved at all times through right and wrong but also teach them how to make right choices.

Also, limit the choices they make on their own. After all, you have more experience and you are the parent!

Child psychologists are learning more and more about the importance of the first five forming years. These are the molding years for a lifetime and golden years for shaping children for life.

Strong decisive parents give children a framework of expectations to work from. This framework is like walls of a home, a safe, secure, predictable place where children emotionally learn security, responsibility, and love.

Teach them right from wrong and how to be a blessing around others and things; a difference they will need for security, responsibility, and love.

Lessons More Powerful Than College Education

Have you been thinking about remarkable education opportunities for children without spending a million dollars for college? Of course, college doesn't really cost a million dollars but it might as well if you can't afford even the college tuition!

The following are themes to teach children right at home for great personal success. It comes from the record of the world's most powerful knowledge, the Bible.

Teach children most awesome respect for God, people, and things. This will enable them to gain respect of their own later in life and grow in leadership, promotion, and pay.

Teach children how to be sensitive and caring to the needs of others. This will enable them to work successfully with others and achieve super bowl type wins because of skill to build teamwork.

Teach children how to be students of the Bible. This will enable them to develop their inner skills to find treasure from a page worth more than all the wealth of the world.

Teach them how to have a walking, talking relationship with God. This will enable them to tap the greatest source of knowledge for answers which are plain, simple, and opposite to the failure of the world.

Jeremiah 17:8

For he shall be as a tree planted by the waters, and that spreadeth out her roots by the river, and shall not see when heat cometh, but her leaf shall be green: and shall not be careful in the year of drought, neither shall cease from yielding fruit.

About family

All good things one could want are found in family! This message shows how to take it all to the top and have it all by bringing it home to family.

It's All About Family

Family is the springboard to launch children into life. The themes children learn in the first five forming years are the groundwork for the rest of their lives.

We are witnessing something never before seen in the history of mankind, all under the watch of the so called intelligent!

For the first time in history, children are being raised outside of the family love. Instead of family, they are getting day care, TV screens, computer monitors, and a world of stranger, too many and too strange to know, and far removed from the family love.

Common trends are raising children with broken love and broken trust. They grow into adults carrying castles walls (insecurity) around their castle hearts to protect themselves from the world of strangers they came to know at day care.

They are selfish because they don't know love. They are isolates because they don't know family. They are lost because they don't know success.

Show children how the family works together. Show them how to solve real-life issues with real family teamwork.

The next message shows how. It is a message about family called, "Keeper of the home". This message, as you would imagine, is opposite to the common culture working opposite to family values!

Keeper of the Home

Keeper of the home is one most potent message with most profound impact upon family life. It shows how to shape family values and family benefits from family livelihood!

What we do with this message will determine the outcome for family and family life!

Since livelihood is the lion's share of time in life, it is also the lion's share of impact upon family. Some livelihoods add greatly to family benefits while others work opposite!

This message empowers in the most positive way because it shows how to build family, family values, livelihood, and prosperity upon the same most powerful prosperity principles and a most outstanding values system – all while we work as keeper of the home!

Remember the old days when America's prosperity system came from the family unit, either from the family farm, or the family run small business? Back then, families lived with, played with, and worked with each other in the family run business. This was their sustenance and it was all about relationships between dad, mom, and kids!

Today's family has changed, and often, we see it is not for the better. This new way finds families all over the nation following a different standard set down by a culture of corporate rules. These demands are coming from corporate headquarters rather than family.

This way is commonly dividing family members from real family themes. Here, families draw sustenance and family practice from the corporate system while losing family time and family values working away from home! The following shows how to take back lost ground with power between the ears.

The answers are found in traditional values and learning again how to do business from home where family themes can thrive once again in the family operated business.

A home-based business can prosper mind, heart, body, family, and pocket all at the same time in ways the corporate system can't. It comes from working opposite to the corporate way.

The opposite of wrong is right! The opposite of failure is success! The opposite of error is truth! The opposite of poverty is prosperity! The opposite of broken families is whole families, happy, healthy, prosperous, and loved.

About Marriage

Man and woman. Two as one! Intimately in love together mentally, physically, and spiritually! One heart and one love connected together in one flesh in marriage. See how nothing is better!

The Golden Standard Of Marriage

A spouse who adores you for life! This is the golden standard of marriage, a standard everyone wants! Here are thoughts to achieve it. Marriage goes where marriage starts. It can start just the way you want it - right from the start.

You know it takes two in marriage, marriage of the body and marriage of the heart.

Marriage of the body is the one many master quickly.

This will be mostly about marriage of the heart for a marriage which lasts; certainly a rare standard in today's marriage and one requiring rare knowledge to do.

The following is rare knowledge for having the love of your heart and a great marriage.

The love of your heart isn't first about who you date. It starts first with you and your perfect standard.

Your perfect standard is completely within you; power to love others and life with full-time love. This love can be with you through every kind of weather and increase the love you receive.

This love is the basis for having a marriage partner who adores you with a marriage of the heart.

It also comes from Him who is within you.

I John 4:7b - 8

Beloved, let us love on another: for love is of God; and every one that loveth is born of God, and knoweth God. He that loveth not knoweth not God for God is love.

Next, it starts with who you date. Fixing a nation's marriage can happen after marriage but an even better place to start is before marriage. Before marriage is where everything starts. Where marriage goes depends upon where it starts.

From the records of the world's most powerful knowledge, we are given reason to build what we do the right way from the start on a solid foundation.

It comes from having a masterful way to think. There is a standard which gives us power to think most masterfully for exceptional marriage. It is found in I Corinthians 3:11 …

No other foundation can no man lay than that is laid, which is Jesus Christ.

He has perfected ways to think and live, ways which lift us to our highest standard.

Through his standards, we can start everything right with the best of everything; but it doesn't happen with marriage to the wrong person with wrong values.

Are we observing the standards or are we saying, "Yes, I do" to something less, and then, paying a price that could cost us for a lifetime?

Keys To Beginning Marriage Right

Marriage is a subject starting with acceptance. Why? Because love starts with acceptance! The best part about marriage doesn't stop there. It begins there before going to a higher standard! Isn't this what everyone wants? To be loved for who we are?

Nothing affects who we are more than how we think. After all, we are the sum total of our thoughts.

The Bible offers us most remarkable material to manage in the mind and heart. This material for the mind and heart serves us in most compelling ways. It is a tangible resource we can read regularly to learn and practice. It includes life's most positive, powerful truths, truths for living life's highest ways.

Another sure way to begin marriage right is to marry someone with values in the most important ways. This way, you can enjoy how the other person thinks for a lifetime.

The next two sections address how to think to have a most fulfilling relationship, a relationship with endearing qualities for a lifetime. These sections also describe tips for selecting the right spouse.

Don't Marry Un-acceptance

Wouldn't you agree, those in our lives who affect us most are those closest to us! The spouse, simply due to such close relationship, is likely to be most influential. The greatest defeats or greatest victories are also shared most with spouse. Is this incentive for making a right choice for marriage which could last for a lifetime?

Consider how easy it is to make a marriage choice because short-terms conditions feel good? But the best decisions are made for the long-run for a marriage that lasts! The right choice will benefit both parties. After all, who wants to be married for a lifetime to un-acceptance?

Consider this before saying "I do!" so both in relationship make a wise choice and not marry un-acceptance.

Un-acceptance appears in many relationships after the honeymoon. It is seen in personal values and in different ways two people think. One thing is for certain. You don't want to marry someone who doesn't accept you and love you for how you think.

Our choice is to make sure we have enough foresight to make the right choice for marriage. This means understanding value differences between two in marriage. Of course there will always be some. The big question is, are the differences acceptable for the marriage you want for life?

Don't marry un-acceptance!

Values For Successful Marriage

Values for successful marriage come from the Bible. This is true for two reasons.

First, there is no better way to enjoy the unity of two as one in marriage when both husband and wife live together from the same common standard. Without one common standard, there is no common union for building life together.

Second, the Bible provides the highest standard for love, union, and insight like none other can.

This is a way filled with positive empowerment, God's love shared between two, and most successful insight from God Himself for a lifetime of marital pleasure!

The Bible's Most Potent Message About Marriage

The most potent message for success in marriage is found in Ephesians, chapter 5.

This record defines God's way to add quality to individuals so individuals can add quality to marriage and get along most remarkably!

Can there be happiness in marriage without happiness in individuals? The Bible has answer for happiness in both.

This standard helps us to see good in life, see good in others, be most thankful, and be most loving in marriage!

Ephesians 5:20 ...

"Giving thanks always for all things unto God and the Father in the name of our Lord Jesus Christ."

The attitude of gratitude is our best state of mind. Thankfulness is the place to start!

The next four verses show how to have harmony through leadership in marriage. Only when leadership roles between husband and wife are understood and in place, can there be harmony in marriage and family.

Ephesians 5:21-25 Submitting yourselves one to another in the fear (respect) of God. Wives, submit yourselves unto your own husbands, as unto the Lord. For the husband is the head of the wife, even as Christ is the head of the church: and he is the savior of the body. Therefore as the church is subject unto Christ, so let the wives be to their own husbands in every thing. Husbands love your wives, even as Christ also loved the church, and gave himself for it;

Men are to act their part as leaders in love. The Bible describes the power and details of that love so men can have that standard to follow.

Also women are to marry men who have these qualities. It wouldn't make sense for a woman to marry a man she didn't respect and couldn't follow.

Christ's love in marriage happens when the man loves the wife as Christ loved the church. This establishes a most compelling pattern of love good for the whole family to follow.

This love in practice is the foundation for perfect harmony in marriage (and family). It starts with perfect love from God and His son. Then it adds strength to the man and woman who follow the example. The standard is made complete in the family with an example for children to follow.

All who know this example can know the greatest love and enjoy the greatest harmony in marriage.

Ephesians 3:18 reads, *"the love of Christ passeth knowledge"*. Every best answer we receive comes to us by love. By living in his love we can come to know everything we need to know to be most successful. When his love is the focus, everything is better.

Our focus on Christ in the spouse in marriage enriches the relationship. This is a spiritual love which comes with spiritual focus. It includes many things to be thankful for including God's way to maximize quality of life in individual, marriage, and family life.

This is the Bible's most potent message about marriage! It shows us how to view Christ in each other in marriage so both in marriage can have unprecedented spiritual love for each other in marriage!

Marriage Starting As Children

Where marriage goes depends upon where it starts. It starts with children in the first five forming years of life.

Unfortunately marriage success for many children is given away in the early years because parents aren't teaching children how to relate. Parents are setting up children in the later years for divorce, broken families, and lonely lives.

Too much TV time and computer time are replacing quality family relationships, events, and quality family love.

Another part comes from in-sufficient love from understaffed daycare workers earning minimum wage.

Neither are children getting what they need from neglected, abused, nasty children which nice children meet at day care.

Divorce rates nationwide now exceed 50%. In California, the state which leads national trends by ten years, divorce rate is at 70%. How long will it take a nation to know things are wrong? All of these broken families, and single parents, and children without parents, are adding up huge failure in crime and violence and broken hearts and much more!

Our whole system requires fixing in order to serve families and every positive theme rather than lose it all to a large failed system. Obviously, the answers are opposite to the greatest failure!

The Culture Of Marriage

Have you found that the culture of marriage today is very different from how it was when marriage success was common? Here is a snap shot view of marriage culture – the way it is compared to what it was when marriage success was common. This message ends with how to return to a common marriage culture which works.

Consider the days on the farm when the only main cultural difference was the difference between male and female. Life was good then because this was a good and common culture.

All over America this culture began with boys and girls working on the farm. They woke to do the same chores which boys and girls did. They fed chickens and milked cows early in the day. They baled hay in the summer and harvested crops in the fall. All of this was similar culture. It was also similar all over America. The work of the day shaped them by similar tasks which all performed daily. There was only one difference. Some were male and others were female and life was good.

Today's culture is very diverse with a great array of differences. The themes shaping culture today vary immensely from the friendly common culture good for male and female relationships.

Isn't it common to find today's culture filled with a world of strangers shaped by different interests and different ways to think? These cultural differences are trouble for those in the realm of dating and marriage.

What is the answer?

There is a culture built on love, gentleness, kindness, honesty, and other desirable qualities. This culture gives those who date and marry the same positive values to think.

These form common ground for those from many walks of life. This is the culture for all time - perfect truth for life from the Bible so all can remarkably be on the same page for common culture which works with universal answers good for all.

This is how to improve the culture of marriage!

About Livelihood

What we do for a living is what we do for life. This is the lion's share of life. Here are ways to add the lion's share of enjoyment to the lion's share of life!

How To Start With Nothing And Build An Empire

No objective could be a more rewarding and no lesson could be more potent! Master this one for everything you could want!

This message shows how to utilize free resources to build an empire without spending a pretty penny! This is an ultimate lesson in resourcefulness for profiting most no matter what you do for livelihood!

First, maximize self by maximizing others!

Play on a team. You are much better gaining from the power of a team versus that which you could gain on your own!

Design a team to function according to your choosing. There is a world filled with talent for a team which serves you best. Choose right talent so you enjoy a winning team with all key players. This also includes another part of success - eliminating from your team those who can't or won't perform! Your life will be much smoother when you build your team with those who share your values!

A few wishful thoughts aren't enough to give you what you want. Instead, employ an entire system so the system lifts you. Let this system engage you, everything you are so you are lifted entirely!

All of the above are available free to all who follow this system!

Start with a blank page so your start has no negative elements. Design your plan your way with only positive parts so your plan is truly great!

Do the above for the long-term and you will master all of them for truly great success!

Do the above to get everything you want! This is how to start with nothing and build an empire!

About Professional Development

Professional development is for the whole person, everything we are and everything we hope to be. This message shows ideas from the highest truth for maximizing self for greatest reward professionally.

How To Maximize Contribution To Self And Others

Professional development gains most by contributing most to others. This is also about the golden rule for richest ways to sow and reap and prosper.

Here it is, a perfect message! What we contribute in the richest ways, we gain in the same remarkable ways because we reap whatever we sow. All we receive and all we could possibly desire comes from what we sow to others.

What is most rewarding to sow? Most rewarding is putting success into words. All of the best can come to us when we know how to do it.

You've heard the saying, "Give a man a fish and he will eat for a day or teach him how to fish and he will eat for a lifetime!"

What could be more potent than teaching how to fish! This happens by putting success into words and repeating success with others! This is the most powerful way to make contribution to self and others and prosper.

P.S. - The way to master success is to share it. The more we sow, the more we reap! This is why the next message is so important!!

P.P.S. - What do you want? Health? Prosperity? Improved relationships? Reap what you want by sowing it!

The next message describes how to share success!

Sharing Success

Have you found your greatest moments happen among friends while putting success into words? Putting the best into words is empowerment at its best! What could be greater? What could be better than putting success into words?

Here are ideas for adding fun and success to life.

Success happens first in the path in the mind. This is where all success begins. Nothing great happens until it starts here! The path in the mind is just like a physical path with the same similar lessons. Consider how easy it is to walk a physical path! The path in the mind, also the path of success, is just that simple!

Just like a physical path, the path in the mind has steps one after another in easy to repeat sequence.

Each step relates to every other and each step brings us further. Visual signs along the way tell us where we are, what path we are on, our location on the path, and what will be the result at the end of the road.

Every path is made this way. Some paths lead to victory and some paths lead to defeat. The results of each are also certain. The path in the mind is the one for shaping the greatest future. It tells us all we need to know!

All in all, the path in the mind is the greatest way to share success. The lessons tell us where to start and where to go. They also teach exactly what will happen at the start, in the middle, and at the end of every road! This is how to share success!

Sharing success is the greatest conversation going!

The Greatest Leaders

Correcting the largest problems is the way of the greatness leaders. The largest problems are so bad no one wants them. They are also so large no one can deny them. The largest problems are beat on the other side with the brightest solutions. The solutions always make most sense!

Overcoming the largest problems is where the greatest good is made. Here, the great become great in solving the largest problems.

The Bible shows how. It shows how to overcome evil with good. These words are the power base for becoming all we can possibly desire. The best happens by living in the greatest good.

The answers are the same for one and all. The key is to master success by putting the best into words. The answer to overcoming the largest problems has always come from words!

The best of success happens first by putting the best into words.

P.S. - Respond to the future even before it begins by positioning yourself on the opposite side of the largest problems. The largest problems are the answer to the best in everything - extreme perception, confidence, and prosperity for how to do things right – opposite to the largest problems. This is where every opportunity is best!

How To Live Like A Billionaire

This message incorporates the truth of the richest verse in the Bible. This verse provides the way to think in our minds in order to live like billionaires and have more than we can ask or think.

The verse is Ephesians 3:20.

Now unto him that is able to do exceeding abundantly above all that we ask or think according to the power that worketh in us.

Most people would be happy if this verse just promised to pay their utility bills. Watch how it does much more! It provides a quality of life and a means to have sustenance more than we could imagine!

We can enjoy this standard by putting into practice this verse and three preceding verses. These verses empower us to achieve what we want. The results come from love!

Ephesians 3:17 *That Christ may dwell in your hearts by faith, that ye, being rooted and grounded in love.*

Christ dwells in us when we believe he does.

Roots hold great trees in place while giving life-sustaining nutrition. So it is with our roots. These are the roots of love. These roots give us great sustenance and help to live like billionaires.

Because billionaires have so many resources, they never have to worry about getting what they want. Love is what we are to be rooted in because love is our answer to living like billionaires and getting everything we want.

Biblical love is the power which prospers us with abundance far beyond all we can ask or think. This love in us works beyond ourselves with higher reach, more productively to benefit others.

No longer should we be in need or worry about ourselves. God has given us the way to live above by finding ourselves richly blessed - above and beyond all we could ask or think according to Ephesians 3:20.

Here is more for achieving the standard -

Verse 18. *May be able to comprehend with all saints what is the breadth and length and depth and height.*

Love inspires understanding so we know the difference between right and wrong, success and failure, and good and evil — all of these so we can make right choices and live in the good with great success!

Verse 19. *And to know the love of Christ, which passeth knowledge, that ye might be filled with all the fullness of God.*

His love passes knowledge regarding all good things we need and want. His love helps us to know what to do in order to accomplish every goal. Every good thing comes with love.

These four verses, Ephesians 17 through verse 20, establish the means to receive the greatest results and the greatest prosperity. This is the way to think and live like billionaires so we have everything we could ask or think.

P.S. - All greatest results come from knowing how to win in a world filled with failure. Here is how. Don't look to the world of poor ideas for answers. Go to the other source, the one who has all the answers and no limits to what He knows! The answers come from God above through Biblical knowledge!

His plans make perfect sense. The details are obviously outside of the box and much better than those inside of the box. These are the only lessons with a full course in winning!

Prosperity Riches

The Bible's prosperity message teaches prosperity answers like no other.

It tells of the sower sowing seed and MULTIPLING harvest! The sower sows a handful of seed in the spring and reaps bushels of harvest in the fall. Our prosperity system can be built to function the same. This section shows how to implement the plan!

It starts by living the golden rule - treating others how you'd like to be treated. There is no apathy here. There are billions of people to help and billions of opportunities to prosper.

Unlike other ways which put limits on income, this way has unlimited prosperity growth.

This way makes people, not things, our business. Isn't this better than making business out of paper, plastic, or stone?

This business builds leaders. Every most successful professional is paid this way. This pattern is not just for an elite few. All who want can employ the same principle regardless of talent! There are resources to help you do it. What you conceive and believe, you can achieve!

Jesus Christ showed how life's greatest opportunities did not come from football, basketball, or catching the biggest fish.

He said, *"Come follow me and I will teach you to be fishers of men."*

Fishers of men do the following.

They build success in others, build winning teams, and surround themselves with winners.

They play the most rewarding game of all. This is the game for keeps, the game of life. They build super bowl type champions and win super bowl type wins. They do so with the world's keenest knowledge and the most powerful principles, principles seen commonly in the best team sports.

Fishers of men have outstanding value to offer and they know it. Their offer always makes most sense both on paper and in practice.

They put into practice all most compelling themes for helping others grow. They develop leaders through teaching, training, and teamwork.

They make it their business to sort wheat from chaff, good from bad, positive from negative, believer from unbeliever.

They sort those who think outside of the box from those who think inside of the box. They sort those who love from those who fear. They sort those who contribute from those who take.

They have strength to stand down any critic with superior knowledge, confidence, and wisdom. They expect to hear from critics and critics don't bother them.

They have remarkable friends who love them because they represent good and spread good like the sower sows seed.

Fishers of men do not cast their pearls before swine. Instead, they work only with people who like what they offer. They keep life simple, untangled, and prosperous.

Life's very best can happen when we make success happen as fishers of men.

We can sow whatever we want and reap whatever we sow. Sowing good to others is the key to receiving all we desire.

Every good thing we desire, all success, comes from relationships. The skills we learn as fishers of men are the same for success in family, friendship, marriage, livelihood, and every subject.

Every theme of life is played out in the world of human experience and we can learn all of them as fishers of men.

Fishers of men overcome the most evil trends with the greatest good on the other side. The most evil trends are so bad no one wants them. They are also so big no one can deny them. Fishers of men compete with the most evil trends where opportunities are best - on the opposite side of bad. Here, the best is available in every way; personally, mentally, physically, spiritually, financially, and more!

This is where the greatest prosperity is. It comes from being fishers of men and showing others how. The world's richest paid people are paid on the talents of others! You can too by repeating the same in a business system which trains people to train people in life's finest truth. This is a prosperity system for prosperity like no other? It multiplies!! All can partake by living the golden rule!!

P.S. – See from this message how the greatest ways to prosper financially and spiritually are exactly the same!

About Prosperity

Prosperity is an outcome and a measure of successful thinking and achievement, a subject of the heart and mind with power to translate success to every realm! It is a course that offers with it, a lesson of unlimited thinking and personal potential, a course for incorporating life's richest lessons about prosperity for prosperity! This course is for prospering in both person and pocket book.

Solving "I can't afford it"

Life's big financial dilemma is such because it is so common. It is so common that people everywhere are saying to themselves, "I can't afford it" even to the most important things and that is the problem. It is a problem because "I can't afford it" takes a grand toll on life in its entirety.

Here is how to do something about it with easy to do lifestyle steps which work to solve the problem.

This way, you will be pleased and not disappointed with the life you lead and your results.

This lifestyle plan is easy to add to any existing plan. It can even replace plans that are not working.

This way, you can prosper and stop saying, "I can't afford it!"

See in the following message the parts of this new prosperity plan.

A New Prosperity Plan

The following is a completely new way to prosper and afford what you want with a completely new way to think and live.

It is completely new because it works opposite to the common plan built the common worldly way. The common plan is built upon love of money, the root of all evil. Many times this common way affects us in ways we do not know.

If you are not prospering the way you think you should, you might have the wrong plan. May you find the following to be helpful for reaping prosperity a much better way!

The new prosperity plan is not new in time since it was the very first prosperity plan ever made. It is the original prosperity plan designed by our maker for all of mankind to enjoy for maximum enjoyment of life and living.

It didn't come by working for money. No, there is a much better plan for the mind and heart and pocket book.

Here are the details.

God said to love our neighbor. He also said the greatest is love. Truth like this makes every realm of life better including our financial life because we are always better for living this way.

One very obvious way to know you could benefit more from the new prosperity plan is if you are continually telling yourself, "I can't afford it" to very important things like health and well-being for you and your family.

III John 2 says, *I wish above all things that thou mayest prosper and be in health, even as thy soul prospereth.* - KJV

These two are most fundamental qualities of life. God has stated His will in III John 2 and He has provided the means to live this way through His prosperity plan.

The following five series show more details of that plan. Be ready for truth's most powerful depiction of prosperity and poverty and how each happens.

Each of these parts was written for answers to poverty, greed, selfishness, indifference, pride, and other evil works.

Have you found that all of life is either about principles of truth or broken beliefs? Regarding prosperity, some work environments in some industries are built upon truth. These make prosperity an honest to goodness opportunity. Others are so messed up, prosperity is either difficult or impossible to achieve.

The original prosperity plan was built before time began. It was built completely by love. It helps us to repeat prosperity and repeat life the way it was meant to be from the beginning - completely by love.

P.S. - My livelihood is love and my sideline is the world's most powerful business! This is the LifeStylers USA Business Motto!

Answer To Indifference

If you've been thinking about implementing powerful prosperity ways, this part shows how - opposite to indifference.

It starts by overcoming evil with good. Identify the evil and there is a better way to prosper on the other side. Our whole system can be built this way in a way that is ALL good!

Two common evils plaguing our nation are insensitivity and indifference. These two are contributing largely to poverty and pain.

The following shows poverty and pain to overcome and ways to overcome them.

Fathers, mothers, sons, and daughters all over America are financially enslaved in inadequate pay plans. As a result, many parents and children are getting far too little time with loved ones.

Approximately 45,000,000 Americans have no health insurance coverage

Moderate to severe poverty awaits over 50% of today's workers in their senior years.

Should we be silent and do nothing as we watch loved ones and nation become sick and buried in debt, or should we be caring and do something to change it?

Doing nothing is the certain way to lose.

Without people to care and help, this pain will hurt.

Caring and healing their pain is the opposite to evil with answers in big demand for prosperity. Here is how to prosper.

Caring overcomes evil with good. Every problem has a solution. Every question has an answer. Every pain has a cure. The answers come from seeking.

Ask and it shall be given you; seek and ye shall find; knock, and it shall be opened unto you. - Matt 7:7

The Bible teaches prosperity through selfless motives. Take care of others for the greatest ways to prosper! This is also the greatest market.

Let no man seek his own, but every man another's wealth.

Selfless motives give perfect perspective of others in order to know the good for healing their pain. This prosperity teaches how to think, live, and share good with others and be in large demand. Without caring, nothing begins and the cycle of prosperity is broken.

Good has the power to attract and be a number one bestseller. It offers more appeal and opportunity for prosperity than all of the competition. The good it brings offers every incentive to seek it and know it more.

For those who seek improved prosperity, the goodness found by caring is an excellent way to prosper. The more we care, the more we know to live in fulltime goodness.

Heavens words are perfect ways to think and live to prosper.

Overcoming Evil With Good

The following is a perfectly powerful way to achieve prosperity financially, personally, and in every way. The logic is taken from Romans 12:10, a model for overcoming evil with good. See perfect sense here for life, livelihood, and prosperity.

This prosperity happens by working opposite to evil. Here's how! Evil is weakness in the process of business because it fails to produce what buyers really want. Therefore, it fails to be an attractive option. But evil is an attractive option to compete with in business because the opportunities on the opposite side are so much more appealing.

The Bible calls love of money the root of all evil. Have you seen it in corporate systems built purely for profit? For systems built this way, profit is far more important than people. As a result, many employed by these systems are feeling the hurt in unhappy work environments which span the globe. The following are just a few of the many ways to compete with evil and win in very large ways.

- Replace systems built by greed with systems built by caring

- Replace systems which tear down by competition with systems that build up by teamwork

- Replace systems that are hectic and hurried with systems that are simple and fun

- Replace low pay income with high pay income which increase every year

- Replace short-term jobs and poverty futures with powerful paying long -term income for life

- Replace work patterns which work for self and limit self with work patterns which help others and help self

These are ways to overcome evil with good to prosper financially, personally, and in every way.

Do you want an excellent model for life and livelihood, one that wins consistently in a world filled with opportunity? You can in a special life style way with a home-based business built the opposite of bad!

This business thrives where traditional corporate business cannot. It thrives in a world of personal service where helping others is the answer to true prosperity. The market for this business is huge and prosperous with little competition. For those who work this way, the opportunities are endless and so is the prosperity.

Take On Goliath Where The Money Is

The end of want! Enjoyment of life! Abundance to conquer evil! Prosperity in the most powerful way - personally, financially, and in every way! Here is how to have it.

Overcome evil with good. Be like David. Take on Goliath.

Beat the world's wealthiest companies where the winning is best. How? By competing with the wealthiest where the wealthiest are weak!

Where are they weak? In exactly the ways which make you strong - like personal caring and service to others, like strength found by developing friendship, unity, and teamwork with others! Like honesty, and integrity, and other positive human qualities people enjoy in others!

In summary, wealth comes from being the best human being you can be, and by doing so, you will be your best in business as well. Why? Because people enjoy doing business with others they like.

Want to be wealthy? It starts with you on the inside!

Jesus Christ said, *"The kingdom of God is within you!"*

We can utilize this kingdom to live in the royal prosperity of God. It comes from overcoming evil with good to prosper.

This is how to prosper and afford life's best. It happens by taking on Goliath.

The Largest Untapped Market

The following answers the question, "What is the largest untapped market and why is this important to me?"

This is important because a large untapped market can be the foundation to great prosperity and quality of life for a lifetime. Sadly enough, many people working in highly competitive markets will have limitations for a lifetime.

A brighter business way starts at the top and grows success in the largest untapped market for maximum prosperity. This market is opposite to the competitive one found in the large global economy.

It is a market of personal service. This is a market where very large companies are not set up to serve. This is a market where large companies cannot compete.

This means the opportunities for prosperity are much greater in this market without all of the competition which most livelihoods experience. This one is also most fun and fulfilling by building life and prosperity in ways which help others most.

Are you looking for a perfect place to plant your life and livelihood to enjoy life and prosperity most?

There is a perfect plan. It benefits in every way including personal prosperity, health, family life, family values, ethics, and much, much more.

How about trading in the old tired market failing to prosper lifestyle? Trade it in like an old, broken down car. This way, you can enjoy a new, completely untapped market with huge financial and personal rewards for the long-run.

These are keys to prosperity.

About Dating

Where marriage goes depends upon where it starts. It starts with dating. About dating shows how to start for shaping one of the greatest decisions of life and the greatest benefits of life-long love.

How To Date For Success In Marriage

Marriage goes where marriage starts. It starts with dating. Here is one way to date for success in marriage. Date different than the common way to make a right choice for life. The following are thoughts for fixing ailing divorce rates.

It happens with marriage to a soul mate, one who loves you for who you are.

Where does it start? It starts by keeping objectivity in dating to find your soul mate!

Objectivity is the first thing needed for dating but many throw out objectivity first.

Dating is often a test in faithfulness but actually this test is a school in divorce. Why? The best way to find faithfulness is to find a soul mate!

Faithfulness is for after you find the right one rather than before. When those who date stay open to what they are looking for, all are served better by right decisions which serve the long run!

Who wants a marriage that feels good before marriage but then, after saying "I do", you find yourself married to un-acceptance? Wouldn't you be better off alone and happy rather than finding yourself married to un-acceptance? After all, un-acceptance puts you in the red!

Un-acceptance happens when one mate doesn't accept the other. That can occur for many reasons. One thing is for certain. Where there is un-acceptance, both in marriage have it because in marriage, two become one.

You don't want un-acceptance for a lifetime do you? This is why it helps to do your homework before marriage so you make the right choice for marriage.

How about keeping objectivity in dating so all can make a wise choice which serves each for life? How about looking for the one you wouldn't trade for any other? Dating is the best way to find out. Would you have it any other way?

Great marriages can happen most frequently with the right way to date.

P.S. - How is this for dating? Be happy with who you are regardless of who you date. Then, all else can go better.

P.P.S. - A date with a friend can be a win regardless of the outcome. This way, a friend is never lost. A date with a friend can also assist for making cool, calm decisions. This is how to know when conditions are right for the ultimate relationship.

A Key To Finding The Right Mate

Find yourself at your best to find the right mate! This simply makes finding the right mate easier.

Start with a great love mission. Find a love mission which cultivates the best in you. By cultivating yourself most passionately, the rest becomes easier!

You will find yourself most happy with you, and you will shine best in the crowd with the best of love within you.

A great love mission can improve your focus on most meaningful values, lifestyle ways you like, and lasting friends who share your values.

All in all, a great way to find the love of your life!

About Sex And Love

Sex and love is the great subject with far reaching impact on every most endearing subject and thought! Use it right and everything can go right! Use it wrong and everything can go wrong! This message offers insights into sex and love so both together can be a most fulfilling couple!

Why Not Do One-night Stands

All successful relationships, all those we want, share intimate trust and trustworthiness. Break that trust too early, and see what you get!

A one-night stand, and close to it, can give the potential love of your life an impression you are easy and untrustworthy! Easy with him/her and probably, easy with others!

You don't want to be married to the love of your life who doesn't trust you do you?

Be smart! One-night stands are everything opposite to what you want in the love of your life. Do it right for a lifetime of love and trust!

P.S. – Waiting to do it right can add value to the relationship and value it more!

The Great Choice In Sex And Love

This message addresses two choices for sex and love and how to enjoy the best choice for the best of both worlds.

First choice – Have hot sex! Get married! Realize afterwards your partner doesn't like the way you think and doesn't accept you either! And then, that person wants to have sex with you? I don't think so!

Here's the second choice. Keep your mind and emotions in-tacked. Be cool, calm, and collected so you come to know your potential spouse for his/her other qualities besides sex.

Nothing could help you more than an objective look at your choice to make a right choice for life.

This is the second choice. If you make the right choice before marriage, you are more likely to have great sex for a lifetime, rather than just for a short time.

How To Have A Great Sex

If you know the statistics, you also know that love life for many heads south after the "honeymoon". For those wanting great sex in a glowing love life, the following may help.

The first sign love life needs improvement comes after the honeymoon. There's the typical attraction until the couple realizes that one doesn't accept the other for how he or she thinks. After realizing this, sex appeal between the two takes on a different view and the relationship loses its glow. No one would want this to happen would they?

Here's how to increase the odds for a lasting relationship and a rewarding sex life. This way can be most endearing. It starts before marriage by selecting the right mate. This is a person who thinks like you and thinks in love.

Lovemaking is like it says. It is about love and how to think in love, not just for spouse, but also for others. Then, because you are all love, the love between two in marriage becomes all that more special.

Our greatest cues for love come from God's example of love. These are found in the Bible.

The Bible is our practical guide for love in every way. It shows how to align our thinking and attitudes in love to love in a most appealing way in every kind of situation. The same also adds sex appeal for being more loving. What could be greater for winning both ways?

This is how to have a great sex!

Great Sex - Part two

To be loved as a whole person - in body, mind, and spirit! What could be greater?

Consider how many lovers would love a passionate relationship like this – to be loved completely for ALL OF YOU!

This message shows how to have it.

The greatest love life happens between two intimately in love in body, mind, and spirit. The Bible shows how with most amazing love so two can be one on the same page with God's love shared between two.

The Bible shows how to think most positive thoughts so lovers can have something most loving to love in the mind, heart, and soul of each other. This includes love, tenderness, consideration, empowerment, and every most positive thought!

The Bible is the book for how to do it and be on the positive side of life, living, and thinking. All of the best happens in the mind in a great love relationship. It happens by the insights of God in the Bible.

Here are remarkable words for remarkable love from Ephesians Chapter 5.

Man, love the woman as Christ loved the church. Woman, submit unto the man as the church was subject to Christ.

Christ's love for each other is the focus. Both the man and the woman can have this focus and find empowerment to love with the greatest love.

Christ in your lover can be the focus and power of your greatest love. Jesus Christ is the hallmark of humanity, every thought, every most kind and thoughtful way. Tap into the passion of Christ for your lover and may his tender thoughtful ways and beliefs be the foundation to your love life.

Love each other with the passion of his love described in the Bible. This is the answer to great sex!

The Greatest Beauty Secret Of All

You already know that beauty is skin deep. Here is the greatest beauty secret of all for shaping beauty inside and out.

It is the beauty each of us can practice on the inside. It is the beauty which makes us all love. This is also the beauty which people seek most in their relationships with others.

You may have heard the expression, "People don't want to be impressed! They want to be appreciated!" Personal beauty happens by showing appreciation for others!

This beauty on the inside is easy to do and most effective to implement for greatest life changing results. The Bible says of all things, the greatest is love. When life is based on perfectly pleasing love, love is the foundation for everything great including beauty!

Love improves us individually. It also improves our performance in everything including personal beauty.

This is the greatest beauty secret of all.

About Personal Achievement

What could be more fulfilling than repeating the greatest patterns of personal success? These are easy to repeat for every most positive result. This message shows how for greatest personal achievement.

The Power Of Common Sense

Will Rogers said, "Just because it is common sense does not mean it is common practice!" Most people would agree, what we need is more common sense and more common practice.

Here are ideas to do it.

When making choices, compare options before choosing. Best is best compared to every other! Find countless ways to make comparisons free! Every way can be tested, weighed, and compared before making choices. This way, the ways we choose are what we know is best before we choose the winners! May you find the following to be that kind of message!

Nothing is more common than personal failure and personal success.

Both are transparent because both are universal to every person. Both also spell success or failure for every person.

Because both are universal, you can spot one or the other in every person you see. This is obvious by how people think, believe, and act.

There are many ways to destruction. You see it everywhere. But the way to succeed is absolutely remarkable. The successful way works for every person.

The patterns in this book are proven ways to do so. This is the power of common sense!

A Plan Worth Giving Our Best

The plan worth giving our best is most logical! Do you have such a plan? Does it earn full conviction because it logically provides the results you want most? The plan worth trusting with full conviction is the plan most certain to give us what we want. Do you have such a plan, a plan worth giving your heart and soul? Half-hearted plans only generate half-hearted conviction, half-hearted success, and lack-luster results.

Success starts with a logical plan! A truly logical plan builds trust, conviction, and belief to receive superb results! Superb game plans produce super results!

Without such a plan, weak conviction breeds mediocrity and life without success.

A successful plan always makes sense on paper before it makes sense in practice - a vital key for real success!

The Power Of The Mind

Scientists claim the mind is a great under-used asset? We can change all of that with improved daily and weekly focus. Consider the power of the mind to help us achieve all we want. It comes from focus on desires we really want!

The Key To Success Is Repeating Success

Every person knows how to repeat success. How many times have you ironed a shirt or swept a floor or completed any menial task? With repetition, the task becomes easy to repeat! All success works just like that. Once we've done it, we can repeat it again for greater success!

All success works this. Success was made by our maker to be simple! All success is ours to have if we will only do it!

The Measure For All Success

Have you found that all success can be measured in tangible terms and then duplicated? Unless a pattern is tangible and measurable, it cannot be duplicated. All success is measurable and can be duplicated!

Repeating Success Makes Fine Improvements

Success comes from repeating success over and over again and fine-tuning to the nearest perfection for most desired results. Isn't it amazing, how much potential we have to improve our ways and results when we apply this simple key?

Practice makes perfect!

About Spiritual Achievement

Values are valuable and add more value to us! They give us desire, reason to pursue, and value by showing us how to achieve.

The Bible is the power book for value, values, and achievement. It speaks more clearly, more compellingly, and more profoundly than any book regarding every life style subject. It is loaded with value, values, and achievement.

Jesus Christ mastered value as he became the author of all achievement. In his profession he was the master of all professions.

He was the master fisherman. He showed how to catch enough fish to fill boats.

He was the master physician. He healed those who were blind from birth.

He was the master builder. He built a building that will never fall.

He was the master businessman. He built a following that would be the envy of the business world.

He taught words which produce wholeness in every profession and in every achievement.

He taught how to believe in value, values, and achievement. With him, all things are possible!

Truth works! Error doesn't!

Truth is the original insight for authentic results. It comes from spiritual focus on spiritual victory won by Jesus Christ. This is the blue print for all achievement.

Truth: The Perfect Life Style Subject

Nothing could be more beneficial and pertinent to lifestyle than truth. Why? Because truth gives most compelling answers for how to think, believe, and live to receive right results. Right results come from thinking right and believing right. Truth teaches how to do it. Truth works. Error doesn't.

The Bible is the book of truth and the book of instruction for life from God to man. This is the source for all potent answers. It includes the ways to think, believe, and live for most compelling results. Without the standards of truth to live by, the ways of mankind are negative and broken with broken beliefs which fail to work. (See II Timothy 3:16.)

Words of truth show how to live by priorities which work so all who desire can start at the top in every situation with best ways to think, believe, and live. (See II Timothy 3:16.)

These are thought patterns established by Jesus Christ. By his example, he showed how these patterns of thought work to overcome every defeat and win every victory. Now that this is done, we have something worth repeating to receive the same great results.

This mindset of victory is not about defeat, worry, frustration, anxiety, poverty, sickness, or any other negative thought. Instead, it is a mind-set only about victory and how to live in victory in every most positive way.

And now, since these ways are completed and perfected, they are ours to enjoy and share with others.

This is a mind-set with power to transform every aspect of our lives into victory simply by the way we think and believe and live.

This is why truth is the perfect lifestyle subject!

How To Know What Is Truth

Truth is perfect words for shaping life the right way with right results. Truth always works. Error doesn't.

Truth incorporates every genuine lesson and every life style topic into one common theme. This way, we can know that God wrote the book on success regarding every life style topic and every way to succeed.

How do we come to know truth? It doesn't come from the common religious way.

Jesus Christ spoke the following words to the religious leaders of his day.

Ye do err not knowing the scriptures, nor the power of God. - Matt. 22:29

Those leaders could not know truth or the power of God because they were filled with preconceived ideas of truth. Was it truth they knew? Not if Jesus Christ was right. This is why he said what he said.

What was their problem? They were already committed to their own religious (denominational) views. Neither were they open to hear more. Because of this, they could not have objectivity or honesty to know truth.

Today, many Christians have the same problem. They don't even read their Bibles, let alone follow it. In addition, they've been reading newly written Bibles and newly written messages which fail the standards of Biblical truth. This is easy to see when what they read is exactly opposite to Biblical truth (i.e. King James) written in plain English.

Wouldn't the words of Jesus Christ be just as potent today when he said, "Ye do err not knowing the scriptures nor the power of God"?

When Christian people know how to read the Bible, they can also know truth in it's splendor, perfection, and power. This is how to know what is truth.

How God Speaks With Us

This is about the greatest lifestyle subject of all. It is about how God speaks with us for perfect knowledge which works the perfect way for life.

The other way, men's way, is filled with imperfection, guesswork, confusion, and argument. But God's way is always perfect.

John 4:24 *God is spirit and they that worship him must worship him in spirit and in truth.*

God speaks spiritually because He is Spirit. He cannot be known by the five senses because He is Spirit.

The Bible tells us in John 1:18, *No man hath seen God at any time.*

The spiritual way to know Him is not by the five senses. He is known by spiritual means and He speaks with us spiritually.

One way comes from simply reading the Bible. This is the first way God speaks with us because His word is His will.

His written words are always the first place to start because the first words given are the first words He wants heeded. Why speak more if the first isn't heeded?

The second way God speaks with us is spiritually, also called revelation.

He speaks by giving us spiritual knowledge and spiritual understanding. We can learn life's ultimate lessons through spiritual talk.

Sometimes He speaks with us to give us more understanding about His written words and sometimes He speaks with us about very practical matters as He give us vital answers. What He speaks will always flow with His written word and never against it or contradict it.

This is how God speaks with us.

How The Bible Interprets Itself

Truth is only as good as ones knowledge of truth and how to arrive at truth.

Presently, people everywhere have broken beliefs regarding God and what He can do for them. They don't know how to communicate with God for anything.

They have broken beliefs because they lack knowledge of His perfect word, which is perfect truth, which reveals God and His ways to mankind.

Before one can trust, truth must be known because truth teaches how to trust.

II Peter 1:20 says, *Knowing this first, that no prophesy of the scripture is of any private interpretation.*

This is the first thing we should know as people of God and people of truth. The first thing we should know is that we are not given right by God to interpret the Bible any way we want according to our private views.

There are three ways THE BIBLE INTERPRETS ITSELF.

1. In the verse - right where it is written

Approximately 85-90% of scripture interprets itself right where it is written in the verse.

2. "In the context" defines the meaning of words in the Bible by how the meaning of words are used in context.

Anything written can be taken out of context to mean something completely different. This happens regularly by those who use the Bible to say what they want it to say. To do so is not honest, intelligent, or right. To understand truth, every Bible topic must be understood in the light of its Biblical context.

3. According to previous usage where the word or words have been used before.

A classic example of this is Paul's thorn in the flesh. There are many contradicting opinions regarding the true definition of Paul's thorn in the flesh but all of them are wrong unless they go back to the first place in the Bible where the term was first used. The first usage reveals the true meaning of the word. Meanings of words can be clarified by first usage.

These keys to how the Bible interprets itself are vital to understanding the Bible and how it applies to life as the ultimate instruction book.

How To Walk In Truth

The following is about a most rewarding life-style topic - how to walk in truth.

God said in I John 1:4 *I have no greater joy than to hear that my children walk in truth.*

Walking in truth is just like walking in a forest. It is all around us. It is a path we walk on. It is constant knowledge to know what is right. It is everything we smell, taste, touch, hear, and see. It includes a constant relationship with God who is always with us to guide us in the highest ways to think, believe, and live to reap the victory He has given to us through His son, Jesus Christ.

In order to walk in truth as I John reads, we must know who we are so we can walk in truth. Truth says we are children. We must know this in order to understand our position in life and how we are to walk as children.

First, we are children of a spiritual Father. When we know that, then we can walk in truth and be spiritual which is the first step to walking in truth. We know who we are.

The second part of our walk in truth is to know our Father, the Father of Truth. We are children and He is a Father. This is why we are called children and this is why I John 1:4 says *"He has no greater joy than to hear that His children walk in truth!"*.

Once we know who we are, then we can know how to walk and where to walk because we have identity.

I Corinthians chapters 12 - 14 are the instructions for all of God's born again children for how to walk spiritually.

(For how to be born again, see perfect words from heaven in Romans 10:9. - King James Version)

We can know these ways and walk in these ways and practice who we are spiritually.

This is how to walk in truth so we can think spiritually, act spiritually, and live spiritually as children of God.

About The World's Most Powerful Knowledge

In this day and age, specialists are common where a lot is known about little and little is known about a lot. The world's most powerful knowledge offers better. It is a brand of knowledge which teaches a lot about a lot. It comes from Him who wrote the book on success. He ties it all together in one awesome lesson. Here, every part contributes to every other and every authentic lesson gains from every other authentic lesson for maximum learning and success! The life style system you are reading from here is such a system. It employs the best of the best which comes with special knowledge, the world's most powerful knowledge. This knowledge ties it all together as one most potent success course.

Speed Learning

Here are simple keys to speed learning.

Learn from committed people. They have found something of great price worth committing themselves to.

Learn from successful people. They have learned how to be successful and can show you how to repeat what is already done.

Be a student until you are filled with everything you can imagine.

Make special time to cultivate your greatest passions.

Love with the greatest love. Love teaches the most valuable lessons, the most dependable lessons, and love passes knowledge.

The World's Greatest Intelligence

The world's greatest intelligence was taught by him who said "Ye shall know the truth and the truth shall make you free!"

He taught the world's most simple truths which relate to every other truth then, tied them all together as one perfect, most dependable doctrine. These are the truths which determine the largest difference for people everywhere.

The world's greatest intelligence starts with the world savior who taught how to be whole and free in every category of living!

His intelligence is made complete in old, and especially, New Testament learning.

I Corinthians 1:27 *But God hath chosen the foolish things of the world to confound the wise; and God hath chosen the weak things of the world to confound the things that are mighty.*

This is the world's greatest intelligence.

Why Educated People Do Dumb Things

In the big wide world of educated people, educated people do really dumb things. Have you ever asked yourself why?

Educated people come from a canned institution of knowledge. Their institution is built on the theories and guesswork of men and often, they consider this to be smart.

Here is the other side of smart. Learn from every lesson in creation and Creator. This is the source of all intelligence. This is learning which doesn't lie and always works in the most real ways as the greatest intelligence. It always works! Every little part and every little lesson works with every other part for real dependable learning and the greatest success in life. To be really smart, add every smallest lesson to the whole where all of the parts work together as a whole for real intelligent learning. No intelligence could be greater than that which ties all of life's themes together in one neat school of understanding.

I don't consider the finest education to come from men's theories and guesswork, and their canned institution of knowledge. Their world is filled with all kinds of imperfect motives. To build a much more intelligent plan, build on the knowledge which ties it all together with real life lessons from life's real great author!

When trusting intelligence in the largest ways of life, how about looking to Creator and real life lessons first!

Knowledge You Can Trust

Truth is always simple, logical, believable, and achievable. It always leads to the most desired finished result, the whole person.

Error is always complicated, hard to understand, hard to believe, and doesn't make sense. Error teaches that success is not attainable.

Every success requires a successful game plan in order to produce successful results. We can require in our personal success plan a game plan which makes sense before we invest our future.

Life's great author wrote the ultimate game plan. It includes the brightest knowledge so even a fool need not error. He authored all success. The plan is both simple and trustworthy. Would you have it any other way?

It starts with truth. Truth teaches how to have trust, confidence, and power to believe so we can achieve and live in wholeness.

Right answers are always simple and flow with every other simple answer. Each simple lesson strengthens every other simple lesson so there is great confidence and full knowledge to know what is right. This is knowledge that life's author wouldn't keep from any soul seeking answers.

In a world filled with doubt, aren't you glad you can have something different? This is knowledge you can trust which always makes most sense!

The Meek Shall Inherit The Earth

We are the sum total of our learning. Everything we receive and everything we become happens because of what we know.

The world's most powerful knowledge teaches everything we could possibly want.

In a world filled with failure, there is victory on the other side. It happens by doing things opposite. Success and failure are always opposites.

The Bible says the meek shall inherit the earth. The meek are those who are open to learn and seek out the learning.

The meek shall inherit the earth is a promise to those who place their minds in the right place to learn.

Consider the possibilities.

Be meek and inherit the earth.

How To Be Happy, Whole, And Complete As One People Of One Nation

The following topics are loosely combined to form one message for how to be happy, whole, and complete as one people of one nation.

The Culture Of God vs. The World

The culture of God is opposite to the common worldly culture. It is a culture built completely for success by Him who is all success. He is, after all, the one who created the heavens and the earth and all success.

His culture teaches how to reap success in everything by right knowledge. After all, how could there be success without first right knowledge?

You will see that the culture of God starts on the inside with knowledge to shape the heart, mind, and attitude right so all things we do can start right and finish right - and build good culture!

The other culture, the culture of the world, isn't working! For example …

Approximately one in every thirty-two people in America now has a home address at a corrections facility.

It is predicted that one in every three babies born in 2000 will have diabetes.

One in two marriages will end in divorce.

Homosexual bumper stickers tell us to question gender as if there is not male and female.

For the first time in the history of mankind, parents are raising babies with TV screens, computer monitors, and low pay day care workers rather than the family unit and family love.

The intellect of the intellects who are driving this system, no matter what kind of titles they have, are not smart because they lack God's knowledge found in the Bible!

All the above cultural trends illustrate that America has lost its way with toxic cultural habits needing desperate change!

America is in trouble! This trouble comes from living priorities of the world outside of the priorities of truth. Perhaps the nation should receive warning labels from the Surgeon General regarding the toxic nature of the world's culture.

How is the culture of God different? First, it is not toxic and complete failure like the culture of the world. The culture of God teaches all of the great detailed ways to be successful in what we produce for human culture so we can build life, livelihood, and all we do his way and reap much better life. First, it comes from love for God and His standards in the Bible and love for others so all we produce is made to serve others. This is God's way for shaping culture. It is not toxic like the other culture. The other way requires us to continually read the fine print to protect ourselves from predators. If not, risk suffering the consequences of falling victim to greedy, self-serving money-grubbers.

The culture of God is built by love to serve life's recipients with the best of life's benefits. It includes living the golden rule. This is, treating others the way we would like to be treated.

This is the culture of God vs. the world!

Where Christianity Begins

Christianity begins with life's most beneficial Bible verse. See in this message why this verse is the first step on the path of Christianity and see why it is the best step to receive everything Christianity offers for a lifetime of walking in truth.

This verse is Romans 10:9. It is a spiritual message about living a completely new and better standard, a spiritual standard, God's standard for life.

That if thou shalt confess with thy mouth the Lord Jesus, and shalt believe in thine heart that God hath raised him from the dead, thou shalt be saved.

This verse includes for every person who accepts it a whole package of salvation and the ability to benefit from virtually everything God has given freely in Jesus Christ.

It includes an attitude to do all we do God's way with an unprecedented victory mind set. Those who live by the personal lordship of Jesus Christ are empowered to shape their minds, hearts, and lives around life's greatest victory, the victory Jesus Christ won for all who believe. This is how winning can become a way of life.

Ephesians 1:3 *Blessed be the God and Father of our Lord Jesus Christ who hath blessed us with all spiritual blessings in Christ.*

Notice the word "hath". Hath is past tense meaning it has already been done for us.

Many of God's people erroneously wait for God to act with blessings and answers for their lives. But actually, God has already provided both through the accomplishments of His son. These accomplishments are written within His word for us to know and enjoy in practice.

And ye are complete in him, which is the head of all principality and power: -
Colossians 2:10

There is nothing more to do to earn more blessings. God through his son has already provided all of them for every person. In order to reap those blessings we must take action to receive them. This is our part.

And be not conformed to this world: but be ye transformed (with a new figure in your mind) by the renewing of your mind, that ye may prove what is that good, and acceptable, and perfect, will of God.
– Romans 12:2

This describes our responsibility to control our minds and thoughts according to truth and act according to truth so we live right, believe right, and receive right results.

Spiritually, we already have the message and truth about how to live in the victory through Jesus Christ.

This is where Christianity begins. It begins with Jesus Christ as Lord. This victory can be a part of our every day life. It can also be our great focus in everything we do. We can do all we do much better this way because we know we have been given all we need in wisdom and understanding and positive ways to live in complete victory.

This is the great beginning of Christianity. It starts with Romans 10:9 by confessing Jesus Christ as Lord.

How To Prosper Through A Christ Centered Life

Get ready for this! It may be the best you've seen for living the greatest life and receiving prosperity based on a Christ centered life!

This is not about boring, negative, life styles or livelihoods which many give their precious lifetime for and complain about.

First, a Christ centered life is not about working for money or pleasing a boss, fulfilling financial obligations, or other worldly priorities for working. No, life is too short for that.

Life is worth much more! The life he gave us to live is about living all of the most important themes first and making all others ways whole in the process. He taught how to build all we do completely by love. This is the love which builds teamwork and harmony. It teaches how to build the right kind of following with just the right kind of people. It is an ideology for making one and all whole with most successful living.

He built the greatest following any man has ever built. His following would be the envy of the business world. The way he built his following is exactly the same way to build prosperity based on a Christ centered life.

See below how to do it.

Be all you can be by being Christ-like to others. This way, you will be loved and respected by many. This is also the way to excel professionally. Why? Because the best professionals are also great people first! "First things first" is the key to greatest success and prosperity.

He used goodness within him to further the success of others. He also built all of his life around the greatest insights of success and he shared that success with others.

The greatest ways to think and live are written in the Bible. Seek Biblical truth with great enthusiasm to learn all you can about wholeness, victory, and love!

Also, enjoy friendship with others who share the love for Biblical truth. Then shape your life by passion as you share the same with others. As you do, you will be most happy with yourself and you will be a positive contribution to others just like Christ was. This is also how to grow prosperity financially in business and in livelihood. It doesn't happen by chasing money or other negative themes.

This is how to prosper through a Christ centered life and live the highest quality of life.

God Doesn't Use You

The Bible proves it. God gives free will so you can be keen as to how to use freedom and live in victory the way Christ came to deliver. The following shows the Biblical logic for why God doesn't use you.

One exceptional place to begin is in Romans 9:10 about salvation wholeness. This is the mother of all subjects relating to free will.

That if thou shalt confess with thy mouth the lord Jesus Christ and believe in thine heart that God raised him from the dead, thou shalt be saved.

Salvation happens by freedom of will. This includes every part.

Also included in salvation is Ephesians 1:3 *Blessed be the God and Father of our Lord Jesus Christ who hath blessed us with all spiritual blessings in heavenly places in Christ.*

This verse clearly tells us that God has already blessed us with all spiritual blessings. These blessings are ours to start using immediately! No longer do we need to ask for them or wait for God to give them to us because they are already ours. We receive them by our freedom of will and by exercising believing faith.

No longer does God want us to wait for His blessings when He has already told us in His word He has given them to us. To wait for God's blessings is wrong believing and a poor use of freedom of will.

The best use of freedom of will happens by managing our minds and hearts to believe and take positive action on the promises God has blessed us with in His word. This is believing faith. This kind of believing pleases God!

Truth shows how to think right, believe right, and receive right results to live in wholeness.

All of the above work by exercising freedom of will. This is why God doesn't use you!

Steps On The Path Of Eternity

In case you have ever wondered what eternity will be like, here are steps on the path of eternity described in Biblical detail

The first step on the path of eternity starts with Romans 10:9.

That if thou shalt confess with thy mouth the Lord Jesus, and shalt believe in thine heart that God hath raised him from the dead, thou shalt be saved

This verse shows us specifically how to be born again to receive eternal life.

Once we are born again, we are given a new way to think and live. This is freedom from guilt, condemnation, shame, sin consciousness, and more! All negative mind-sets have been replaced by a very positive achievement. This achievement is every most positive thought, emotion, and result in salvation. Spiritually, because Christ did what he did, all negative thinking has been replaced. Why? Because Jesus Christ paid the price for all sin. By accepting him as Lord, we also accept the work he accomplished including payment for sins. Spiritually we are sinless and this is how he wants us to live. It starts by thinking his way! This aids "sinless" living, opposite to guilt and shortcomings.

After this life, the next life will be greeted with rewards, not judgments. Many Christians erroneously think they will be judged, yet, judgment is reserved only for those not born again. Those who haven't accepted Christ will be judged. All Christians however have already been judged righteous (without sin) in Christ.

Psalms 103:12

As far as the east is from the west (the two never meet), so far hath he removed our transgressions from us.

(Also see Romans 3:21-22.)

For Christians, earthly life will end at the return of Christ. Then, two events will occur. First, those have died will rise again. Second, and in order, those who are alive and remain shall be caught up together to meet Christ in the air at his return.

I Thessalonians 4:13-18

But I would not have you to be ignorant, brethren, concerning them which are asleep, that ye sorrow not, even as others which have no hope. For if we believe that Jesus died and rose again, even so them also which sleep in Jesus will God bring with him. For this we say unto you by the word of the Lord, that we which are alive and remain unto the coming of the Lord shall not prevent (precede or go before) them which are asleep.

For the Lord himself shall descend from heaven with a shout, with the voice of the archangel and with the trump of God and the dead in Christ shall rise first:

Then we which are alive and remain shall be caught up together with them in the air: and so shall we ever be with the Lord. Wherefore comfort one another with these words."

These words are a wake up call to Christians. Why? It is obvious from this teaching that mainstream teaching is not consistent with what you've just read in Bible verse. This also means Christians are thinking in error. Mainstream teachings leads people to believe that upon death, the dead go immediately to the heaven. This is not what the Bible says.

Christians have much more to gain by heeding the doctrine of God. It is obvious they are not reading the Bible as they should.

When Christ comes back, all who sleep shall be awakened just like all awaken after a good night sleep. For those who sleep in Christ, the next conscious moment will be the return of Christ and that will be a great moment! See what comes next.

I Corinthians 15:52-54

In a moment, (in a split second) in the twinkling of an eye, at the last trump: for the trumpet shall sound, and the dead shall be raised incorruptible, and we shall be changed.

For this corruptible must put on incorruption, and this mortal must put on immortality.

So when this corruptible shall have put on incorruption, and this mortal shall have put on immortality, then shall be brought to pass the saying that is written, Death is swallowed up in victory.

O death, where is thy sting? O grave, where is thy victory?

I Corinthians 15:57

But thanks be to God, which giveth us the victory through our Lord Jesus Christ.

Philippians 3:21

Who shall change our vile body that it may be fashioned like unto his glorious body, according to the working whereby he is able even to subdue all things unto himself.

We will have perfect bodies like the glorious body of Jesus Christ after he was resurrected from the dead. These new bodies will have far more capabilities than the bodies we have now in this life. All of us will be proud of our bodies because they will be perfect.

Romans 9:33

...and whosoever believeth in him shall not be ashamed.
In the next life, there will not be one part of our lives or one part of our bodies that we will be ashamed of. We have a perfect life to look forward to because none of us will be ashamed of anything.

If we could be ashamed, eternity would not be a perfect place would it?

The Bible tells us in Isaiah 65:17 ...

For behold, I create new heavens and a new earth and the former shall not be remembered nor come into mind.

God in His goodness will take away all negative memories, all guilt, all shame, and every negative thought so all of eternity will be perfect and completely enjoyable throughout eternity. We won't be bringing any emotional baggage with us.

Verse 18 continues ...

But be ye glad and rejoice for ever in that which I create: for, behold, I create Jerusalem a rejoicing, and her people a joy.
And I will rejoice in Jerusalem, and joy in my people: and the voice of weeping shall be no more heard in her, nor the voice of crying.

There won't be anything more to cry about! Can you imagine how wonderful that will be for every child of God?

The Bible also tells us in Isaiah 65:25 ...

The wolf and the lamb shall feed together, and the lion shall eat straw like the bullock (cattle).

There won't be predators in the next life. There won't be the strong preying on the weak. There won't be people lying, stealing, cheating, or taking advantage of others.

I Corinthians 2:9

But as it is written, Eye hath not seen, nor ear heard, neither have entered into the heart of man, the things which God hath prepared for them that love him.

These are steps on the path of eternity.

How To Get Everything You Want With Love

What could be better than a life built completely by love? Love not only works to make us feel good but love is also the ultimate key for success in everything. See why Biblical truth teaches to love for ultimate success in everything!

The most potent love is God's love taught in the Bible. This is a uniquely special love. It works God's way and with God's power and effectiveness. It loves completely unconditional. This love working in us comes from knowing how God loves us.

Have you found that many of life's largest opportunities come from people – pay raises, more job opportunities, more commission, more appreciation from others who like to say thank you? All of these and more come to us by love. God placed His love among us to be shared among us so our relationships with others can be optimal. This is also how we prosper more along the way.

God provided love as the means to live to the fullest. Love in practice leads us to greatest success. It includes loving others His way unconditionally. When our love is unconditional so is our quality of life!

I John 4:20 *If a man say, I love God and hateth his brother, he is a liar: for he that loveth not his brother whom he hath seen, how can he love God whom he hath not seen? And this commandment have we from him, That he who loveth God love his brother also.*

Love is the greatest opportunity of life. It is the one most beneficial way to think and live to benefit self and others most.

Here are details about love to energize our way with top results.

Love God and Biblical truth. The greatest lessons and growth originate here. Biblical truth is the perfect way to think and live. Consider this the "rush to quality" like no other way to grow!

Love others as you want to be loved!

Love everything you want because whatever you love will come to you!

Love shapes our best behavior and gives us greatest results!

Love is the greatest way to excel in every way!

Without love, we are nothing!

With love, we can be everything and succeed in everything!

Love is the greatest way to achieve our best in everything!

The Bible tells us in James 1:17 that every good and perfect gift comes from above. Philippians 4:19 also tells us all of our needs have been supplied in Jesus Christ. What more can we ask? What more can we love?

Above all, love is the greatest!

This is how to get everything you want with love!

The following are answers to life's largest question, how to be born again to have eternal life, as well as relating subjects.

How To Be Born Again

Answer: Romans 10:9 *That if thou shalt confess with thy mouth the Lord Jesus and shalt believe in thine heart that God hath raised him from the dead, thou shalt be saved.*

What Happens To Those Not Born Again

Answer: Those who decide not to accept the spiritual victories of Jesus Christ, and his lordship, die without spiritual benefit. Just like any other creature, they simply return to dust. This is fair. Nothing given! Nothing gained! That is fair!

What happens to the born again after they die the physical death?

Answer: They "sleep in Christ" as the Bible describes until Christ returns to gather them up. I Thessalonians 4: 13 – 18 *"But I would not have you to be ignorant, brethren, concerning them which are asleep, that ye sorrow not, even as others which have no hope.*

For if we believe that Jesus died and rose again, even so them also which sleep in Jesus will God bring with him.

For this we say unto you by the word of the Lord, that we which are alive and remain unto the coming of the Lord shall not prevent (precede) them which are asleep.

For the Lord himself shall descend from heaven with a shout, with the voice of the archangel, and with the trump of God: and the dead in Christ shall rise first:

Then we which are alive and remain shall be caught up together with them in the clouds, to meet the Lord in the air: and so shall we ever be with the Lord. Wherefore comfort one another with these words.

Whose Responsibility Is It To Lead Others Into The New Birth

Answer: God gave that responsibility to His born again children. Responsibility is a part of life. God made it this way.

I Corinthians 5:20 tells us, "*Now then, we are ambassadors for Christ*" We are responsible to do the work of Christ while he is away. As born again children, we are given responsibility to be ambassadors for Jesus Christ. In order to fulfill that responsibility, God has given us the ministry of reconciliation and the means to carry it out. He did so by also giving us the words of reconciliation so we can have the greatest words to say to fulfill that ministry of reconciling others to God.

II Corinthians 5:18-19 *And all things are of God, who hath reconciled us to himself by Jesus Christ, and hath given to us the ministry of reconciliation: To wit, that God was in Christ, reconciling the world unto himself, not imputing their trespasses unto them: and hath committed unto us the word of reconciliation.*

Living In The Power Of The Lordship

Receiving salvation wholeness in the new birth is only beneficial for the next life UNLESS we live in the power of the lordship in THIS life. Then, the best can happen through this lordship! By living in the power of the lordship in this life, there are unprecedented benefits in every way.

This message shows how to live in the power of the lordship to enjoy life's most unprecedented benefits.

Jesus Christ said, "*If ye continue in my word, then are ye my disciples indeed; and ye shall know the truth, and the truth shall make you free.*" - John 8:31b-32

The lordship of Jesus Christ is free from every deception, defeat, disappointment, and inferior way. This is how those who live in the lordship can enjoy unprecedented benefits. The unprecedented benefits come from living in a way greater than our own. This is Christ's way. He made the model for unprecedented benefits in every way! Among others, he showed how all things are possible to those who believe. He also showed how to receive answers to prayer. He also showed how to receive everything we need according to his riches! All we can imagine has been provided in that lordship.

Here is how to live in the lordship! Replace ways which don't work with his ways that do! His ways are superior in every way!

He said, "If you continue in my word!" ... This is better than our way!

The greatest reason for personal failure is self inflicted - self-centered, self-indulgent, self-willed, and self-defeating behavior. His way is our way to a better focus! If we continue in his word, then we are his disciples (discipline followers) indeed. By following his way, we are sure to overcome the most common failure, which is self-inflicted.

"And ye shall know the truth." His truth is the highest of all ways. We were born without answers. He was born to give us answers. We were born without discipline, direction, or love. He was born to give us all of them!

He concludes this verse by saying, *"and the truth shall make you free!"*

This is also our way to greatest success and freedom from every negative thought!

This is how to live in the power of the lordship and enjoy all of the unprecedented benefits of salvation wholeness in this life and also in the next to follow. It happens by continuing in HIS word!

How To Live Spiritually

Spiritual living is just like living any secular profession. An artist paints pictures. An accountant keeps books. A nurse does nursing. And so it is spiritually. In order to live spiritually, we must operate spiritual functions and spiritual abilities to be spiritual.

God who is Spirit (John 4:24) has given us ways to function spiritually with spiritual abilities in order to live spiritually. These are similar to functions in the physical realm except that these are spiritual.

Some of these functions include praise, two-way communication, encouragement, inspiration, exchange of knowledge including exchange of divine secrets, and more. These spiritual functions enhance relationship with God and are vital to spirituality.

Knowledge of these is covered in I Corinthians chapters 12 –14. These are directions for how to live spiritually. God makes it clear in verse one of Chapter 12 that he doesn't want us to be ignorant of spiritual matters.

The Bible shows us how to live spiritually.

The Benefit Of Prayer

The benefit of prayer offers the greatest course in personal development through partnership. Prayer is partnership with God of the highest kind.

We talk with him about what we've received, wholeness, and we talk with Him about how to bring wholeness to pass. This exchange of ideas is directed toward our highest achievement - complete in Him!

The more we talk with Him, the more we perfect our conversation skills and recognition for all we have and all we can be.

Prayer is the most positive conversation going. It offers unlimited potential to do the impossible. It also adds fun while doing it.

Prayer helps to give us direction to realize our greatest achievements.

Prayer puts every subject into focus by putting love into words. Pray much! Love much!

All of life's greatest achievers talk with God in prayer.

This is the benefit of prayer.

How To Pray

There are two ways to pray.

I Corinthians 14:15 *What is it then? I will pray with the spirit, and I will pray with the understanding also: I will sing with the spirit, and I will sing with the understanding also.*

This page only addresses the question, how to pray with understanding. The next subject below addresses how to pray and/or sing with the spirit.

Prayer with the understanding is our way to put our finest into words. This includes everything most important including our concerns, achievements, and everything we could possibly desire.

The best happens by putting success into words. Nothing happens until we do. Prayer with the understanding facilitates everything best we can understand. The more we talk with God about our heart-felt questions, the more He gives us answers.

Prayer with the understanding is our greatest way to think, especially when we align our thinking with God.

This is a large step for how to think and a major step to personal victory - to think the perfect thoughts of God!

This is how to pray with the understanding.

Always pray to the Heavenly Father because you are a child and He is your father. This father - child relationship is the model and most potent lesson for all families everywhere, physically and spiritually. Always pray in the name of Jesus Christ. He is our advocate with the Father and our model for a son.

Always be thankful for all you have and all you want. All of it has been given freely through God and His son!

Ephesians 5:21 *Giving thanks always for all things unto the God and Father in the name of our lord Jesus Christ*

The second way to pray is spiritually as mentioned in the above verse in I Corinthians 14:15. See the answer to spiritual prayer on the next page.

How To Pray Spiritually

Spiritual prayer is perfect prayer. It happens by praying spiritually.

I Corinthians 14:15 *What is it then? I will pray with the spirit, and I will pray with the understanding also: I will sing with the spirit, and I will sing with the understanding also.*

Speak and sing syllables in prayer to God. These are not the syllables you normally speak. These are perfect, not because the words are perfect but because the heart and the spirit are.

The apostle Paul, who wrote most of the revelation of the New Testament, led the way for the perfect heart and the perfect spirit. He said, "I thank my God, I speak with tongues more than ye all." Paul spoke in tongues.

Speaking different syllables in another tongue is the perfect way to pray not because the words are perfect but because the heart and the spirit are.

God wants us to know who He is just like any parent would. He wants us to know all that He is, all the good He can do, and how He works spiritually. He is spirit and He wants us to be spiritual.

God is spirit and they that worship him must worship him in spirit and in truth. John 4:24

All parent wants to be known by their children. God is no different. Because He is spirit, He has provided spiritual functions so we can know him spiritually and have full relationship with Him spiritually. This is the way to know him and have the world's most powerful knowledge.

This is why we can pray perfectly. It is not because we are perfect but our hearts and spirit can be. We trust in Him who is spirit. With Him, all things are possible!

God has all the answers. By aligning ourselves with Him spiritually, we receive His answers and His power. This is the power which makes us victorious and free!

This is how to pray spiritually.

How To Function Spiritually

Spiritual functions are from God to us for having spiritual relationship with Him. These functions enhance relationship. How to enhance spiritual relationship with Him is similar to how we enhance relationship with others.

This includes such relationship enhancing functions as praise to Him for His goodness, two way spiritual communications with Him for gathering spiritual answers, and answers to operating spiritual power and ability. All of these enhance relationship. All of these are answers to functioning spiritually. Biblical instruction for how to function spiritually is found in I Corinthians chapters 12 – 14. This is God's instruction to New Testament believers to be spiritual.

Chapter 12:7 *But the manifestation of the Spirit is given to every man to profit withal. For to one is given by the spirit the word of wisdom: to another the word of knowledge by the same spirit; To another faith by the same Spirit; to another the gifts of healing by the same Spirit; To another the working of miracles: to another prophecy; to another discerning of spirits; to another divers kinds of tongues; to another the interpretation of tongues; But all these worketh that one and the selfsame Spirit, dividing to every man severally as he (each man) will.*

This message continues with an analogy easy to understand. It shows how spiritual functions are many with one purpose just like the body has many functions with one purpose.

Verse 14 *For the body is not one member, buy many. If the foot shall say, Because I am not the hand, I am not of the body; is it therefore not of the body?*

The message goes into greater detail but you get the message!

Spiritual answers are just like physical answers. They are used to enhance relationship. The functions of the spiritual are also good. God is light and in Him is no darkness at all. Therefore, our spiritual functions must be consistent with God's purpose which is all good.

All spiritual people throughout time who have operated spiritual power have operated one or all nine of these. These make up God's spiritual package of spiritual power. Not one more function could be added to make this package more spiritual.

What could be greater than to have relationship with God, the creator of heavens and earth? This is relationship with Him who is also our Father!

This is how to function spiritually.

Overcoming Religious Extremism

Religious extremism is the product of ignorance, ignorance of truth.

The worst religious extremists are those who think they have answers yet they don't. Religious extremists have strayed away from, or never had the logic of life to begin with that God originally wrote as one truth for all of mankind.

Religious extremists can even originate from the fold of God.

Jeremiah 2:13 says, *For my people have committed two evils; they have forsaken me the fountain of living waters, and hewed them out cisterns, broken cisterns, that can hold no water.*

When people forsake the truth of God for ideologies and religions of men, they also forsake the truth of life.

Jesus Christ said this regarding truth, authentic Biblical truth. *"These words are spirit and they are life!*

Christians share the greatest responsibility for either sowing discord or unity. They hold within their grasp the greatest book of harmony and unity among men. So often, however, they choose another doctrine based on religion rather than Biblical truth.

Should they sincerely want harmony and unity, see the two pages in this book entitled "How The Bible Interprets Itself" and "Separation Of Church And State". The right ways have the power of God to bring harmony and unity to mankind. They also overcome religious extremism through right Godly education.

Truth works. Error doesn't. Those who know truth also understand how life works in order to live successfully. Those who don't are deceived into thinking they do but, their ideas don't fit into the real functions and blessings of life. These are religious extremists.

The answer to overcoming religious extremism is to sow truth so ignorance is exposed and replaced with truth. Truth always makes sense and always works to produce what people really want most including harmony and unity among men! Education is the key to overcoming religious extremism!

P.S. – If Christ's lordship was really practiced among Christians, they would all function as one in one body of Christ with Christ as the head. This would be different than being divided by many denominations. Also, they would be the most powerful people on earth with his insights. He revolutionized the world once and his insights can do it again when Christians know and practice what he said!

The Difference Between Truth And Religion

Truth is perfect knowledge from God. Religion supposedly represents God but fails in many ways to do so because it has elements of hypocrisy from man-made ideas.

Truth reflects the perfection of God. Religion reflects the ways of men and has error in it.

Truth always works. Religion only works part time because it only has part truth. The part of religion that works is truth.

Truth is the foundation to every subject. Religion addresses some subjects with truth but can't put it all together because it lacks continuity with all of life's subjects.

Truth magnifies the power of God. Religion reveals the weakness of men.

Truth emphasizes the correct operation of free will. Religion does everything it can to manipulate and control.

Truth comes from knowing how the Bible fits together with the perfection of God without contradiction. It also fits into the entire master plan of life without contradiction so all who know it can apply it to any realm and every realm of life and be successful everywhere. Those with religion seek to protect and maintain their own denominational beliefs and are not open to anything more.
Truth is a way of a Father with his children.
Truth has an unlimited supply of resources from God. Religion has man made limitations and is in fact, a broken cistern.

Jeremiah 2:13 *For my people have committed two evils; they have forsaken me the fountain of living waters, and hewed them out cisterns, broken cisterns, that can hold no water.*
This is the difference between truth and religion.

How To Reach The Goal

The goal to restore the greatest nation is reached just like every goal is reached. It is reached by taking simple steps forward. These are the same simple steps of success that are required to reach every goal. This goal includes protecting our national borders and our national economy so those within our economy are being served. This is better than managing a global economy which cannot be managed. Every goal needs a path to follow and a sequence of steps to reach it. For us as Americans, that means taking steps in the right direction until the goal is achieved. The opposite of failure is success! The opposite of error is truth! One path does it all. This is the path of truth made by the God the Creator of the heavens and the earth found in Biblical knowledge. Every step can be a step in the right direction with the most profound results on the other end for making one and all whole as one people of one nation. America's plan was built upon words from God in the Bible - one nation under God indivisible with liberty and justice for all. Obvious to all who know this way, it is a way filled with the richest human values which attract people to work as one for the highest cause of love for fellow man. This love is far greater than earthly wealth or possession. This path of love is also the key to wealth and possession in physical possessions in order for one and all to be whole and complete and not selfish. The path of truth is the way to achieve every goal. Every goal is achieved simply by choosing a path and following the steps to get there. Restoring the greatest nation is conceivable, believable, and achievable. This is how reach the goal!

P.S. - The most certain way to reach the goal is to overshoot it. For those who give little, little is gained. For those who give much, much is gained. Give much and gain the greatest achievements! This is how to reach the goal and live again in the nation of our dreams, the nation which serves the people's state! All working together in a nation of 300 million is all that is needed. It doesn't take all 300 million. Just enough from that group can do enough to energize the right movement! The other way, idle response, is total failure and underachievement!

Conclusion

The pages of this book were written for a most positive conclusion that God's intelligence is the answer to solving America's problems. This intelligence is far greater than all of the scholars and politicians in Washington combined. He has all of the answers for saving America and every soul from every nation! He is after all the maker of all success! He doesn't look at problems and think they can't be fixed. He looks at problems and has the finest answers! This book was largely inspired by His intelligence found in His book, the Bible. This knowledge is validated by every lesson learned from every subject of life because He has created every subject. More important however, the Bible by words says it best. God knows exactly the words to write and exactly the order of the words that will have maximum impact upon every soul, our ways, and our results. Every failure comes from following all of the words other than His. Likewise, every success comes from following His because He is God and the author of all success. *Returning to America* is about returning to Him, the one with all of the answers. Here all men are created equal and with certain unalienable rights given by God to enjoy life, liberty, and the pursuit of happiness – opposite to the ways of evil men bent on manipulating and dominating the rights of others for selfish, greedy, and destructive gain. To all who love freedom, *Returning to America* is the answer with answers that are simple, within our grasp, and given by God in all of His power and goodness.

About The Author

Mark Dean's passion is putting success into words for life-enriching results. He is a marketing pro, national sales leader, life coach, business coach, and Bible teacher. Twice he received recognition for being among the nations most accomplished sales leaders. Several times he has brought start-up businesses to the top of the class. Over his lifetime, he has been practicing a most potent message which ends controversy with much more appealing results. His number one mentor is the world's most influential leader, the world savior. His number one book is the Bible. This is also his source for intellect and confidence that America can be profoundly improved by the greatest intelligence and the ultimate offer!

The 2007 Petition for America

America's 300 million-majority have power over 536 failed politicians in Washington by repeating one voice together. This petition is one voice for doing so. The other choice is to sit idle while life for self, family, country, and all of freedoms children sink to the worst poverty conditions and everything you don't want by idle response!

This petition may be copied and enlarged on 8 ½ x 11 or LARGER. For the whole game plan for deep reform in America, go to:

www.USAFreedom.us

Current direction in America requires one president, each senator, and each member of congress to vote on each issue of this petition and then make that vote most public. A "yes" vote on all of these issues together is worth 100 points, a perfect score! Each "no" vote loses thirty points. One "no" vote shows serious credibility issues. More than one "no" vote is a failing grade, making that public official unfit to serve the people's state. No response is also a failing grade. We the people demand resignation for any who fail the grade.

End corruption in government within one year! Gain the unified support of all elected officials to do so and end the transfer of America the beautiful from a people's state to a corporate state and then to a foreign state led by communist China. Prevent America's worst nightmare before it happens. This petition calls for immediate and unconditional response to restore America's majority power base! Also, change direction from obvious greed, corruption, and destruction of the land of the free. The details in this petition contain the answers for restoring the power of government of the people, by the people, and for the people as defined in the U.S. Constitution. Any less response will be considered failure and continuation of the current power grab. Current direction led by the few is destructive to the future for all Americans. Our leaders are failing to protect America from greed and greed has far reaching destructive power! Failure to stop this is foolish on the part of the few because the few are no match for China's military based communist ideology. It is time for answers to restore the greatest nation in every significant way opposite to every failure and expense.

Yes _____ No _____ Vote to replace privately funded campaigns with publicly funded debates. This will immediately put an end to the influence of big money over the people's government. Do this in 2007 so the people can have a real presidential election in 2008 with new direction not paid for by big money. Big money has no place in America's politics! Publicly funded debates will provide equal opportunity for all who run for office. Candidates should be elected for intellectual content rather than the current plan only giving opportunity to an elite few who have no answers. Publicly funded debates will open the door to those with the brightest answers rather than ruling them out for not being one of the few. Not only will this end corruption in campaign financing but it will also provide a non-biased, publicly paid way to choose most viable candidates. The real issue is not who wins. The real issue is saving America from a ruthless system of exploitation by the few, communist economics, and perhaps even communist rule down the road! We need right leaders to do that.

Yes_____ No_____ Also end all broken parts of the broken election system. The broken parts only accommodate the few transferring the power to communist China. This includes the two-party system, the Federal Elections Commission, and the electoral college. America needs intelligent answers far more than two failed parties. This petition calls for America's elected officials to immediately fix the election system by remaking a representative form of government for 2008 elections. Open the elections system to those who desire to represent the majority. Do so by simplifying the election system so a representative form of government is restored. Support equal, fair, and non-discriminating treatment of candidates without discrimination based on race, religion, party affiliation, or economic net worth.

Yes _____ No_____ Also talk of treason for those in government responsible for selling the people's state to a corporate state and a foreign state for personal gain. Slavery to a political or corporate system is not acceptable. Neither are tyrants from either Washington or communist China acceptable. Talk of treason will change direction in Washington FAST. Talk of treason will end most corruption in government within one year so change occurs FAST opposite to rule by tyrants.

To restore the greatest nation, we the people demand intelligent response and not failure from our elected officials. Elected officials must end corruption in government as well as exploitation by corporate rule and/or communist military rule.

Yes____ No____ Vote to restore America's majority and maintain a respectable minimum wage while balancing the other side of the equation. To do so, right legislation and taxation must remove greed as an incentive by those exploiting the system. Without balancing both sides of the economic equation, the system remains unbalanced.

Yes ____No____ Vote to support a self-sufficient national economy with the goal of producing most of our own commodities right within our own economy. This will also insure fair trade practice. That happens among neighbors within one economy. Fair trade can also occur with other nations when other nations manage fair wages. Fair trade cannot occur when workers are exploited by substandard wages. Vote to be self-sufficient without having to rely on countries we don't trust.

Yes ____ No ____Vote manufacturing back into our national economy again. Without ability to produce and work and be self-sufficient, intelligence is gone, so are work ethics, and so goes our nation into a state of ignorance, failure, poverty, and economic slavery to those who desire to exploit large majorities through human economic slavery. Vote to rebuild America's manufacturing infrastructure so America is functioning as an intelligent, responsible, and self-reliant nation once again. Make significant steps to do so now so significant progress is made within twenty years.

Yes ____ No ____ Vote to favor U.S. made and operated companies for the purpose of serving America and free world democracy as oppose to favoring exploitation and slave labor conditions and wages. Vote also to support small business, family business, family practice, and family living. This can happen by favoring small business over large business. Currently, those in Washington are favoring large business.

Yes _____ No _____ Vote to protect America from individuals and/or organizations working to sabotage the sovereign interests of the U.S. This should include revoking professional licenses of individuals within those organizations who work against sovereign interests - organizations like the U.N. and the Civil Liberties Union.

Yes _____ No _____ Vote to implement term limits for both the senate and congress. Term limits remove incentive to repeat what career politicians are repeating most, which is voting to preserve their careers and self interests. Term limits will add more constructive competition to the political arena with ideas and values which are needed for dramatic change opposite to the status quo in Washington. Term limits for those in office is required in order to gain fresh choices different from those in Washington selling us to communist ideals.

Repeat each year a new petition for America and a Walk for America regarding new issues. This will be a solid step for all who love freedom!

P.S. - To find out more about the 2007 Petition for America and the Walk for America calling for deep reform, go to: www.USAFreedom.us or find at your local bookstore the book, "Returning to America", the book that will change America by author Mark Dean.

Goal: 40 million signatures by September 15, 2007 and millions more after that!
All doing a little will do a lot!
Mail signed petitions to:

TEAM USA, LLC
PMB 351
N112W16298 Mequon Rd
Germantown, WI 53022-3306

Petition for America Signature Page

Must be a legal US citizen.
This page my be copied and ENLARGED on 81/2 x 11 or larger.

Print NAME, ADDRESS, CITY, STATE, & _SIGNATURE_

1. _____
2. _____
3. _____
4. _____
5. _____
6. _____
7. _____
8. _____
9. _____
10. _____
11. _____
12. _____
13. _____
14. _____
15. _____
16. _____
17. _____
20. _____
21. _____
22. _____
23. _____
24. _____
25. _____
26. _____
27. _____
28. _____
29. _____
30. _____
31. _____
33. _____
34. _____
35. _____